John Imrie

Songs and Miscellaneous Poems

John Imrie

Songs and Miscellaneous Poems

ISBN/EAN: 9783744775960

Printed in Europe, USA, Canada, Australia, Japan

Cover: Foto ©Thomas Meinert / pixelio.de

More available books at **www.hansebooks.com**

SONGS

AND

MISCELLANEOUS POEMS

BY

JOHN IMRIE,

WITH

MUSIC AND ILLUSTRATIONS

AND AN INTRODUCTION BY

G. MERCER ADAM, TORONTO.

$1.50.

TORONTO:
IMRIE & GRAHAM, 26 & 28 COLBORNE STREET.

1891.

Entered according to Act of Parliament of Canada, in the year 1891, by IMRIE & GRAHAM, in the Office of the Minister of Agriculture, Ottawa.

CONTENTS.

CONTENTS.

AUTHOR'S PREFACE..	vii
INTRODUCTION, BY G. MERCER ADAM	ix
PATRIOTIC	19
LOVE, HOME AND FRIENDSHIP ..	85
MISCELLANEOUS POEMS ..	149
SACRED COMPOSITIONS ..	267
SONNETS	292
ALPHABETICAL INDEX	342

THE friendship of the good and true
    Is more to me than gold,
And while I welcome one that's new
    I'll treasure well the old ;
Old friends are like the goodly tree
    Whose leafy branches throw
A grateful shelter over me
    When adverse winds may blow !

FRIENDS dead and gone, friends far and near,
    Friends tried and true, friends ever dear,
Though sundered far, yet all are here—
    Close to my heart ;
And all along life's rugged way,
The smile of Friendship crowns the day,
And hearts are young, tho' heads be grey ;
    Friends never part !

MUSIC AND ILLUSTRATIONS.

LIST OF
MUSIC AND ILLUSTRATIONS.

ILLUSTRATIONS.

	PAGE
PORTRAIT OF AUTHOR	FRONTISPIECE.
NIAGARA FALLS	27
QUEENSTON HEIGHTS	39
THE DYING SCOT ABROAD	48
A KISS THROUGH THE TELEPHONE	119
NATURE'S TEMPLE	161
LIFE'S PROGRESS	172
THE YOUNG MUSICIAN	199
SHE PAYS HER DEBTS WITH KISSES	201
HIS ONLY PAIR OF PANTS	222

MUSIC.

	PAGE
FAIR CANADA	21
SONG OF FREEDOM	22
QUEEN VICTORIA'S JUBILEE	36
SONS OF SCOTLAND	41
SWEETEST WORD ON EARTH IS HOME	50
MY HEART IS SCOTLAND'S YET	54
SONS OF ENGLAND	62
THE BRITISH ARMS	66
CANADA	72

MUSIC AND ILLUSTRATIONS.

MUSIC.—*Continued.*

	PAGE
SCOTCH DAINTIES	80
THE STAR OF LOVE	89
THE HUMBER "FAIRY"	94
A SOUVENIR OF LOVE	96
EYES THAT SPEAK OF LOVE	100
"PAPA'S PET"	115
A KISS THROUGH THE TELEPHONE	116
I MISS A DEAR FACE	134
MOTHER'S VOICE	140
A CHRISTMAS CAROL	162
SONG OF THE DRUMMER	171
KNIGHTS OF PYTHIAS	195
THE YOUNG MUSICIAN	196
YACHTING SONG	218
SABBATH CHIMES	236
MY PORTION	278

PREFACE

TO THE SECOND EDITION, 1891.

It is with mingled feelings of humility and gratitude to my friends and patrons that I pen this short preface to the second edition of my Poems. It is but three years since I ventured to test the purchasing appreciation of the public by publishing my first volume, and now with more confidence is sent forth a larger edition of the same book. My first volume extended to 210 pages; in this edition, containing later poems, there are 350 pages. Acting on the advice of friends, there will be found a number of songs set to music, the melody of which I have introduced as a relief to the eye, and a solace to the ear, of my musical patrons. Most of these songs have been published from time to time in sheet-music form, and have met with a ready sale. The children of the home—as in the first edition—have a liberal share of my thoughts in happiest moods, and I am not ashamed to own that I have as great pleasure in serving them as "Children of a larger growth!" My style

PREFACE.

is simple, but none the less sincere, and my chief desire is to please, and encourage the toiling masses. That these humble heart-thoughts and aspirations for the present and future welfare of my fellow-countrymen, and humanity at large, may be accepted in the kindly spirit in which they have been composed, is the earnest wish of

              Yours, very truly,

                      JOHN IMRIE.

INTRODUCTION.

INTRODUCTION TO FIRST EDITION,

BY

G. MERCER ADAM.

AMONG the diverse interests of this restless money-grubbing world, there is one which should hold a larger place than it does in the affections of the masses,—namely, the honest, unaffected love of home and home pleasures. In these days we are all of us too much disposed to seek enjoyment abroad, and to figure more than is good for us in the eye of the public. The craving for excitement has made us impatient with home, and the fireside and domestic shrines have in large measure lost their attraction. We are no longer satisfied with the novel, with the song or with the play, that used to delight our forefathers; nothing so simple and innocent would now content us. Even our religion has suffered a

INTRODUCTION.

change. The stern morality and unbending creeds of other days have become pliant and yielding, while compromise and emasculated beliefs have taken their place. The old doctrines familiar to the by-gone pulpit now offend us, though we are not particular if the preacher resorts to irreverence and slang,—on the contrary, we rather encourage him in this propensity.

With tastes and cravings so destructive to the spiritual life, what wonder that simple joys and quiet domestic pleasures have in the social world lost much of their charm? Yet "the common people,"—as the phrase goes—the men and women who are doing the every-day work of this toiling world, stand more than ever in need of rest and quiet, and the kindly solacement of happy fireside intercourse. Innocent delights, restful pleasures, and the blissful contentment of a well-ordered, comfortable home, with such intellectual recreation as these Edens afford, must be the necessities, we should think, of those at least whose lot is a ceaseless round of toil. To such our author comes with his tuneful lyre and sings us the gladsome lays of the home and the fireside. Benefactor is he not, to you and to me, if he beguiles us from our distractions and cares, and leads us to realize that after all the world's happiness lies in the quiet comforts and refining influences of home?

INTRODUCTION.

It would indeed be difficult for thoughts, however expressed, on Love, Friendship, Home, and kindred topics, to fail of finding response in the human breast; and the average reader who follows the bent of his own unperverted taste, and is as indifferent to the critics as the poets themselves, will find much to please him in the book. Of profit he should also find much, if his sympathies are as keen and broad as the author's, and his appreciation equal to his, of the warm-hearted Christian brotherhood, and unaffected moral purpose, which should find expression in all our work.

Not its least merit, it must be said, is the fact that there is not a puzzling or baffling line in the book. This should be counted for something, when there is so much in our modern verse, not ambitious of fame merely, but cold, meaningless and empty. The volume is chiefly noteworthy, however, not only for unassuming sincerity on the part of the writer, but for its appeal to the universal and easily-awakened feelings of our common humanity. The unobtrusive piety and strain of religious sentiment which run, like threads of gold, through the book, will, we are sure, not the less endear the volume to the reverent reader, and to those whose hearts have felt the influences of the Divine.

May it be its mission to keep alive the love

INTRODUCTION.

of home, to minister to minds distraught with toil and care, and among its readers — we trust, of all ranks and conditions of men — to implant an eternal Sabbath in the heart.

184 SPADINA AVENUE,
　　TORONTO, ONT.

PATRIOTIC.

Patriotic.

OUR NATIVE LAND—FAIR CANADA!

GOD save our native land,
Free may she ever stand,
    Fair Canada;
Long may we ever be,
Sons of the brave and free,
Faithful to God and thee,
    Fair Canada.

Fair as an opening flower,
Planted in Heaven's bower,
    Fair Canada;
Here many nations dwell,
Loving their freedom well,
Reaping where forests fell,
    Fair Canada.

Land of great inland seas,
Swept by the mighty breeze,
    Fair Canada;
Reaching from sea to sea,
Great will thy future be,
Land of the brave and free,
    Fair Canada!

Land of the prairies wide,
Stretching like ocean's tide,
    Fair Canada;
Land of green hill and dale,
Mountain and pleasant vale,
Here worth shall never fail,
    Fair Canada!

Come, then, from many lands,
Brave hearts and willing hands,
    To Canada;
Come where rich virgin soil
Waits to reward your toil,
Share in the harvest spoil
    Of Canada!

* FINALE.—" God save our Gracious Queen,
    Long live our noble Queen,
        God save the Queen;
    Send her victorious,
    Happy and glorious,
    Long to reign over us,
        God save the Queen."

---

* This "Canadian National Song" may be sung to the air of "The National Anthem," the first verse of which would be very appropriate as "a finale" to the above composition.

PATRIOTIC.

FAIR CANADA.

1. God save our na - tive land, Free may she

ev - er stand, Fair Can - a - da;

Long may we ev - er be Sons of the

brave and free, Faith - ful to

God and thee, Fair Can - a - da!

PATRIOTIC.

SONG OF FREEDOM.

FREEDOM'S glad song we sing;
Free as a bird on wing,
Free as the sweet, pure air,
Free as the sunlight fair,
Shout Freedom's holy song:—
We nothing fear but wrong;
For Freedom, God, and Right,
We'll nobly stand and fight!

While life and strength remain
We will our rights maintain;
Our hardy sons of toil
Shall guard their native soil:
From every hostile foe,
From traitors lying low,
From all that dare oppress,
Our swords shall find redress!

We shed no craven tear,
No tyrant's threat we fear;
Before no foe we fly,
We dare be free—OR DIE!
To death we only bend,—
Our foe, and yet our friend;
The watchword of the free
Is:—"DEATH OR LIBERTY!"

WELCOME HOME, BRAVE VOLUNTEERS!

Song of Welcome, sung by the School Children at the City Hall, Toronto, in honour of the Volunteers' return from the North-West Rebellion, 1885.

WELCOME home, brave Volunteers!
    Welcome, welcome home!
Gone are all our anxious fears,
Answer'd now our pray'rs and tears,
Welcome home 'midst ringing cheers,
    Welcome, welcome home!

Welcome to our loving arms,
    Welcome to your rest;
Welcome home from war's alarms,
Safe from death and all that harms,
Victory hath crown'd your arms,
    Welcome to your rest.

Canada is proud of you—
    Soldiers brave and true!
Ye have dar'd to win or die,
Ye have made the rebels fly,
Let your standards wave on high,
    Soldiers brave and true!

PATRIOTIC.

Welcome home, though wounded sore,
    Battling for the right;
Dreadful marches now are o'er,
Safe from deadly bullets' pour,
Silent now the cannons' roar,
    Heroes from the fight!

Welcome home, but some we miss,
    Brave hearts, where are they?
Gone where noble spirits are,
Gone beyond the reach of war,
Sleeping peacefully afar,
    'Neath the sod and clay.

Welcome home, our soldiers dear,
    Welcome, welcome home!
Rebel threats no more we hear,
War's alarms no more we fear,
Now we smile and dry the tear,
    As we welcome home!

NIAGARA FALLS.

OH, Niagara! as at thy brink I stand,
   My soul is filled with wonder and delight,
To trace in thee that wonder-working Hand,
   Whose hollow holds the seas in balance light!

Worthy art thou to be a nation's pride,—
   A patriot's boast—a world's unceasing wonder;
Like some bold monarch calling to thy side
   Subjects from every clime in tones of thunder!

Deep on my soul thy grandeur is impress'd,
   Thy awful majesty—thy mighty power—
Thy ceaseless tumult and thy great unrest,
   Like nations warring in dread conflict's hour!

Rainbows of glory sparkle round thy shrine,
   Cresting thy waters with effulgence bright;
And in thy foaming currents intertwine
   Rare coruscations of commingl'd light!

Like roar of battle, or like thunder's call,
   Thy deep-toned echoes roll with solemn sound;
Like pillar'd clouds thy vapours rise, and fall
   Like sparkling pearls upon the thirsty ground!

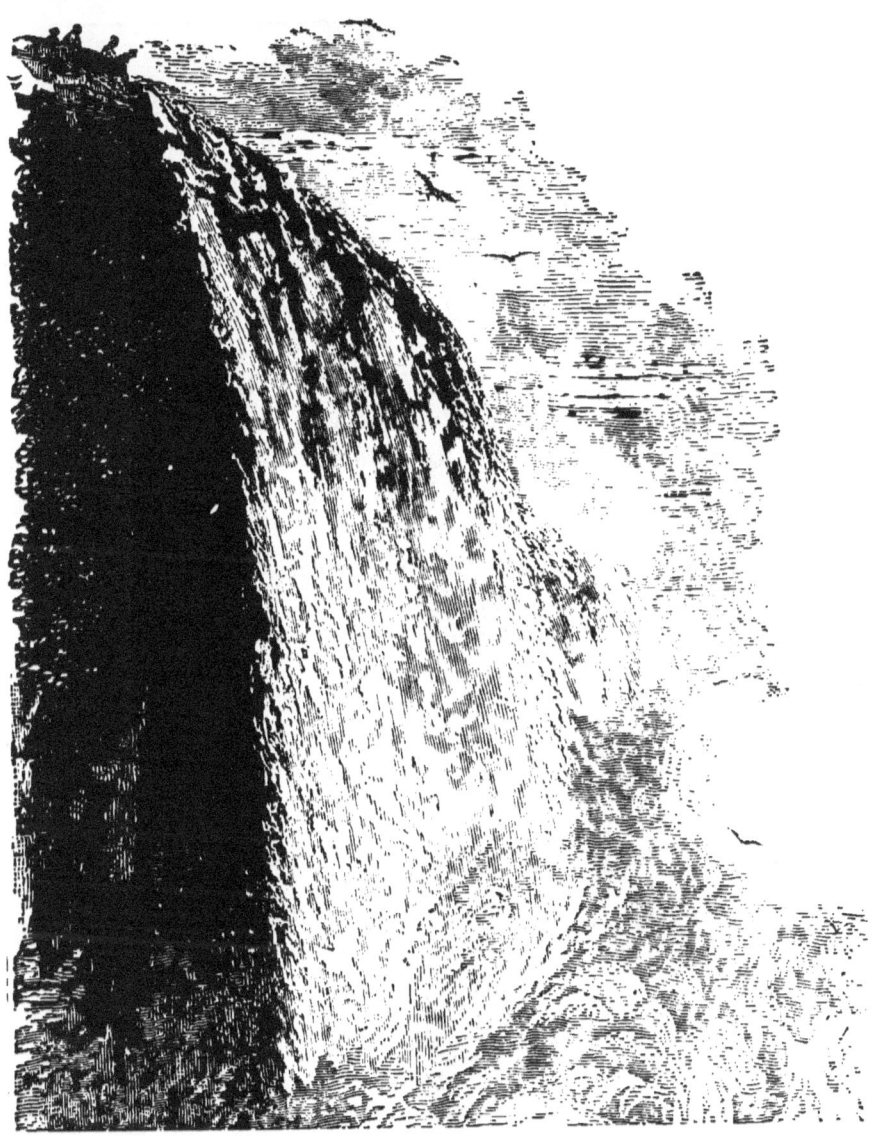

NIAGARA FALLS.

Naught but the hand of God could stay thy course,
  Or drive thee back to Erie's peaceful keep;
Then onward press with thy gigantic force,
  Till in Ontario's bosom lull'd to sleep!

Emblem of Freedom! who would dare essay
  To bar thy noisy progress to the sea!
Then onward press! while bord'ring nations pray
  For strength and wisdom to be great and free!

PATRIOTIC.

Rush on ! rush on ! in thy uncheck'd career,
    With avalanchic power thy course pursue ;
While rending rocks quake as with mortal fear,
    And stand in awe to let thy torrents through !

Naught but the hand of God could stay thy course,
    Or drive thee back to Erie's peaceful keep ;
Then onward press with thy gigantic force,
    Till in Ontario's bosom lull'd to sleep !

Emblem of Freedom ! who would dare essay
    To bar thy noisy progress to the sea ?
Then onward press ! while bord'ring nations pray
    For strength and wisdom to be great and free !

PATRIOTIC.

THE LINKS THAT BIND US.

OH! the fond links that bind us to this earth,
　　Strong as bands of iron—yet fine as gold;
Partings and tears oft mingle with our mirth,—
　　If loving much love never can grow cold!

Ah! were it not for partings now and then,
　　Love of home and friends were never tested,—
Hardship and trial make the noblest men:
　　Present pain is future joy invested!

The patriot's wistful eyes are dimm'd with tears
　　When parting from his much-lov'd native soil,
His heart doth throb with many doubts and fears,
　　Yet hope points FORWARD though his soul recoil!

But when the weary years have come and gone,
　　And o'er the sea he homeward ploughs his way,
He finds his former doubts and fears have flown—
　　Midnight with him hath changed to dawn of day!

A mother parts with one—her only son,
　　Each shews but half the anguish that they feel,—
The voyage finished, or the battle won,
　　What depths of love the meeting doth reveal!

Methinks such joy is ours when God, at last,
　　Shall find us gather'd 'neath Heaven's azure dome;
Our journeys, tears, and partings of the past
　　Will be as naught if we but reach our home!

THE DOMINION OF CANADA.

AN HISTORICAL SKETCH.

"ONLY a few acres of snow!"
 Our country first was styl'd,
By French explorers long ago,
 In winter bleak and wild.

An hundred years roll'd on apace,
 Again they sought our shore,
As summer beamed with smiling face,
 Inviting to explore.

The noble Champlain and his band
 On Quebec's height did raise
The flag of France, with eager hand,
 'Mid thankful prayer and praise.

They fought and toil'd for many years,
 And till'd the virgin soil,
Till happy homes dispell'd their fears,
 And fortune sweeten'd toil.

Grim War again chang'd peaceful scenes
 To carnage and dismay;
But British prowess intervenes,
 And finally holds sway.

PATRIOTIC.

Then hand-in-hand, a peaceful band,
  The Briton and the Gaul
Agree'd to sub-divide the land,
  Together stand or fall!

May peace and honour ever keep
  The brothers thus entwined;
With patriotism—pure and deep—
  Fidelity enshrined!

At last, like fair unfolding flower,
  The New Dominion stands,—
Upper and Lower Canada
  Embrace with loving hands!

Thus July first of every year,
  Our great Dominion Day,
Her loyal sons hold ever dear,
  In honour and display!

The fairest flower on this fair earth,
  The freest of the free;
Whose sons are proud to own their birth,
  And claim their homes in thee!

CANADA'S DEFENDERS.

Written on the occasion of the return of our brave
Volunteers from the North-West Expedition, 1885.

HOME again our Volunteers,
Home again 'mid ringing cheers
Vanishing our anxious fears,
    Canada's defenders ;
From the scenes of strife and war,
From the rifle-pits afar,
True as steel or Polar star,
    Canada's defenders.

Back to home and kindred dear,
Back to lov'd ones waiting here,
Back from death and every fear,
    Welcome, brave defenders ;
Ye did make a noble stand,
Under Middleton's command,
For the honour of our land,
    Welcome, brave defenders.

Welcome back to peace and joy,
Welcome back to your employ,
Rebel threats no more annoy,
    Canada's defenders ;
Stretching wide from sea to sea,
Canada may boast of thee,
Soldiers daring, brave, and free,
    Canada's defenders.

PATRIOTIC.

Let us join the merry throng,
Welcoming with shout and song,
Singing praises loud and long,
    To our brave defenders;
Ye have made the rebel Riel,
Cower 'neath your charge of steel,
Own your pluck, and then appeal
    To our brave defenders.

"SCOTTY."

YES! ca' me "Scotty" if ye will,
For sic' a name can mean nae ill,
O' a' nick-names just tak' yer fill,—
    I'm quite content wi' "Scotty!"

To be a Scot is nae disgrace,
Maist folk can trust a guid Scotch face,
He's never lang oot o' a place,—
    The honest, faithful "Scotty!"

A Scotchman has the knack to plod,
Through thick an' thin he'll bear his load,
His trust is aye in richt an' God,—
    The perseverin' "Scotty!"

He's 'tentive baith to kirk an' mart,
To friends he's true an' hard to part,
In life's great race he needs nae start,—
    "I'll win or dee," says "Scotty!"

PATRIOTIC.

An' if he meets wi' ane or twa
O Scotlan's sons when far awa',
They'll 'gree like brithers ane and a',—
    A " clannish " man is " Scotty ! "

Though aft he travels far frae hame,
He's aye a Scotchman a' the same,
An' prood to crack o' Scotlan's fame,—
    A loyal son is " Scotty ! "

Should Scotlan' ever need his help,
He'll gie her enemies a skelp,
An' make them howl like ony whelp,
    And gie respect to " Scotty ! "

Then ca' me " Scotty " if ye will,
Nick-name like that can mean nae ill,
I'll shake yer han' wi' richt guid will,
    Whan ere ye ca' me " Scotty ! "

QUEEN VICTORIA'S JUBILEE.*

Copyrighted.   Music by Prof. J. F. Johnstone.

Our no - ble Queen, all hail! On this thy Ju - bi - lee;

True hearts shall never fail To love and hon - our thee.

Vic - to - ri - a, to thee, From loy - al hearts and free,

At this glad time, from ev'-ry clime, Come shouts of Ju-bi - lee.

Vic - to - ri - a, to thee, From loy - al hearts and free,

At this glad time, from ev' - ry clime, Come shouts of Ju-bi-lee.

* Lines in honour of the 49th anniversary of Her Majesty's accession to the Throne of England, June 20th, 1837; thus 1886—87 may be termed "Queen Victoria's Jubilee," and all loyal subjects will rejoice with her on whose Dominions, it is said, "*The sun never sets!*"

PATRIOTIC.

QUEEN VICTORIA'S JUBILEE!

OUR noble Queen, all hail!
  On this thy Jubilee;
True hearts shall never fail
  To love and honour thee.
    CHORUS.—Victoria, to thee!
        From loyal hearts and free,
          At this glad time,
          From every clime,
        Come shouts of Jubilee!

From every land on earth
  Thy sons send greetings full,
And proudly own their birth
  Beneath thy sovereign rule.—CHORUS.

In many scenes of life
  Our hearts round thee entwine;
As mother, Queen, or wife,
  Thy virtues nobly shine.—CHORUS.

Let rebels point with scorn,
  Or cowards quake with fear,
Thy true sons—British-born,
  In memory hold thee dear.—CHORUS.

God spare thee many years,
  In trouble send relief;
At last a nation's tears
  Shall wet thy grave in grief!—CHORUS.

QUEENSTON HEIGHTS.

A VERBAL PICTURE.

OH! that I had the artist's power to touch
  The speaking canvas with a master-hand,
I'd paint a scene I truly love as much
  As any landscape in this fair new land!

That picture would be Queenston's lovely height,
  'Neath which Niagara's rushing waters gleam,
Like molten glory in the sunset bright,
  Or fancy's vision in a pleasant dream!

Here two great nations meet as if to kiss,
  Divided only by a silver line;
Peace, welfare, harmony, and mutual bliss
  Link fruitful branches of a parent vine!

The setting sun would tint Niagara Town
  With gilded glory as he sinks to rest;
A noble steamer bearing swiftly down
  Toward Ontario's heaving, billowy breast!

The stately monument of Brock would stand
  In bold relief against the azure sky,—
The valiant leader of a noble band
  Who for their country's honour dar'd to die!

A picture thus I'd paint in Nature's praise,
  And worship at the threshold of her door;
Before the scene I stand in rapt amaze—
  In silence dumb—yet love it all the more!

QUEENSTON HEIGHTS.

Here two great nations meet as if to kiss,
Divided only by a silver line;
Peace, welfare, harmony, and mutual bliss
Link fruitful branches of a parent vine!

PAGE 80.

SONS OF SCOTLAND.

Respectfully dedicated to Robert Burns Camp, No. 1,
S. O. S., Toronto.

SONS of Scotland! land of freedom!
   Sons of noble sires, all hail!
Let your watchword aye be "Freedom!"
   You shall evermore prevail!
Let the wrong be deeply hated,
   Let the right be prized like love,
Martyr-courage unabated,
   Trusting in your God above!

Sons of Scotland! bards historic
   Sang your deeds of noble fame,
Let not tyranny plethoric
   Tarnish your unsullied name;
History gives us what we cherish,
   Ours to still maintain the right,
May that history never perish,
   Though we perish in the fight!

Like the waters from our fountains,
   Giving strength to flesh and bone;
Like the thistle on our mountains,
   Harmless, if but let alone!
Ours to shield the needy stranger,
   Ours to put the erring right;
Ours to stand in time of danger,
   And, if need be, ours to fight!

SONS OF SCOTLAND.

Dear old Scotia! land of flowers,
　　Land of mountain, hill and vale,
Land of sunshine, shade and showers,
　　Land of river, loch, and dale;
Land of ever-changing beauty,
　　Land of liberty and love;
Scotchmen! tread the path of duty,
　　Till you reach the land above!

PATRIOTIC.

ODE TO LAKE ONTARIO.

THOU inland sister-sea, Ontario !
   To glide upon thy bosom is sublime;
There note thy peaceful, steady, onward flow,
   Ceaseless and constant as the course of time !

Thy waters seem the same,—yet ever new—
   Fed by a thousand streams on either side ;
The same clear sky, the same thy depths of blue,
   Free as the nations bord'ring on thy tide !

Vast upper-lakes feed thee with lib'ral hand,
   From higher lands as new as thine hath been ;
Where still the Indian and his wigwam stand,
   He half amaz'd with what his eyes hath seen !

To thy embrace—like gallant lover bold—
   Niagara rushes in his mad career,
Till tir'd and spent, past whirling eddies cold,
   He calmly sinks to rest when thou art near !

Last of the inland seas !—yet nearest home—
   Thy waters soon shall swell the mighty deep,
And mingle with the ocean's briny foam,
   There shalt thou rest—and there for ever sleep !

THE THISTLE.

"NOW, why do Scotchmen use the Thistle
  As emblem of their country dear;
A useless plant, with many a bristle,
  One scarce can touch without a fear!

"There must be some good cause, I gather,
  Why such a flow'r should be their pride;"
I ask'd the question of my father,
  But he my ignorance did chide!

"My boy, let history truly tell,
  Of by-gone years of war and strife,
When noble sires fought long and well,
  And for their country gave their life!

"O'er flood and field, o'er brake and fen,
  The fierce invader sought our land;
Out-numbered were our gallant men,
  But, ah! they made a noble stand!

"One morn, before the break of day,
　　Our foes crept near our slumb'ring camp;
They might by stealth have won the day,
　　Did not one on a Thistle stamp!

"A cry of pain our sentries heard,
　　A quick alarm then was given,
At once each gleaming sword was bar'd,
　　And backward Scotland's foes were driven!

"Since then the Thistle is our pride,
　　'*Gae, touch me if ye daur,*' it says;
And Scotchmen true, where'er they 'bide,
　　Revere the Thistle all their days!"

TO GLASGOW, SCOTLAND.

DEAR Glasca! aft I think o' thee,
  An' happy days lang syne,
Though distant, thou art dear tae me,
  By memory's sacred shrine;
Aft hae I clim'd Balmano's steep,
  An' ran doon Portlan' brae,
An' gather'd "gushes" in a heap,
  Wi' mony a gled "hurra!"

In summer time, whan schule was out,
  An' we had got "the play!"
I've wannert mony a mile about
  The hale lang simmer's day;
A favourite place was Glasca Green,
  By bonnie banks o' Clyde,
Where Nelson's monument is seen,—
  Our hero an' our pride!

An' aft we went by Broomielaw,
  Tae Renfrew's cosy toon,
There mony a noisy luckless craw
  We manag'd tae shoot doon!
Then ower the Clyde, tae Kelvinside,
  We took oor hameward way,
Weel pleased tae ride tae whaur we'd bide,
  Sae tired were we that day!

PATRIOTIC.

Oh! Glasca, dear! I've drapt a tear
  O' happiness an' joy,
At a' thy memories sae dear
  Whan I was bit a boy!
Three thoosan' miles are stretch'd atween,
  My new hame an' my auld,
Yet in my heart sweet memories green,
  S'all bide till I'm deed cauld!

THE DYING SCOT ABROAD.

"Ah, me! ah, me!
An' maun I dee,
Sae far frae kith an' kin;
How prood I'd be,
If spared tae see,
The lan' my heart bides in!"

THE DYING SCOT ABROAD.

"Ah, me! ah, me!
 An' maun I dee,
Sae far frae kith an' kin?
 How prood I'd be,
 If spar'd tae see
The lan' ma heart bides in!

"I've wannert far,
 In peace an' war,
An' fought for Scotlan's Queen,
 Yet here I dee,
 Sae far frae thee,—
Saut tears fill up my e'en.

"Dear freens an' kind,
 Please bear in mind,
An' send this message hame:
 My mither dear
 Wad like tae hear—
I trust in Jesus' name."

'Mid friends' sad sighs
 He clos'd his eyes,
And pass'd from earth to Heav'n;
 Yet, e'en in death,
 With latest breath,
His thoughts to "HOME" were giv'n.

THE SWEETEST WORD ON EARTH IS HOME.

Copyrighted. Music by Prof. J. F. Johnstone, Toronto.

1. The sweet-est word on earth is home, To lov-ing hearts most dear;...... Where-'er our foot-steps seek to roam, Home thoughts are ev-er near.... The mem'-ries sweet of life's spring-day Keep fresh and green for ev··er, Like fra-grant flowers, they scent the way A-down life's wind-ing riv-er.

CHORUS.

The dear-est spot be-neath the skies Is that we call our home! ....'Tis there we look with longing eyes, Tho' o'er the earth we roam.

PATRIOTIC.

THE SWEETEST WORD ON EARTH IS HOME.

THE sweetest word on earth is home,
　To loving hearts most dear;
Where'er our footsteps seek to roam,
　Home thoughts are ever near.
The mem'ries sweet of life's spring-day
　Keep fresh and green forever,
Like fragrant flowers they scent the way
　Adown life's winding river.

CHORUS.—The dearest spot beneath the skies
　　Is that we call "our home!"
　'Tis there we look with longing eyes,
　　Though o'er the earth we roam!

Our homes may be where mountains rise
　Like dark-green clouds to Heaven;
Or where the valley-lily lies
　Our humble lot be given;
Or on an island of the sea
　Oft by the tempest prest:
No matter where our homes may be,
　To each that home is blest.

The strongest love within man's breast
  Is love of life and home;
Like fledglings hovering round their nest
  Our thoughts encircle home;
Our years may reach three-score-and-ten,
  And full of changes be,·
Yet scenes of home will haunt us then
  When life was pure and free.

Where love hath cast her golden spell
  And kindest deeds are done,
Where loving hearts unite to dwell,
  'Tis heaven on earth begun;
Then cherish home with jealous care
  And let not strife prevail;
Thus for our "heavenly home" prepare,
  Secure within the vail.

PATRIOTIC.

MY HEART IS SCOTLAND'S YET.

OH, weel I loe the Scottish tongue,
  The language o' my hame,
An' weel I loe a sang that's sung
  In praise o' Scotland's fame;
It mak's me think o' happy days
  An' scenes o' beauty rare,
There's something in my heart that says:
  There's nae lan' half sae fair!

    Chorus.—My heart is Scotland's yet,
        Though I bide ower the sea:
    I never can forget
        The lan' sae dear tae me!

When travelin' in a foreign lan'
  I hear a Scottish voice,
Instinctively I gie my han',
  An' baith o' us rejoice;
An' then we crack o' Scotland's fame,
  Recite her battles ower,
An' feel we yet could daur the same
  Our faithers daur'd before!

    Chorus —My heart is Scotland's yet!

MY HEART IS SCOTLAND'S YET.

PATRIOTIC.

Oh, Scotland is a bonnie place,
  Wi' scenery sublime;
Whaur Nature smiles wi' fairest face
  That stan's the test o' time!
Each mountain, river, loch, or glen,
  Are fu' o' storied fame;
Wha reads the history o' her men
  Can ne'er forget their name!

    Chorus.—My heart is Scotland's yet!

In every lan' roun' a' the earth
  Are leal hearts true tae thee;
An' prood are they tae own their birth
  Ayont the wide saut sea,
Whaur towers the mountains bold an' gran'
  Like guardians o' the free,—
Oh, here's my heart, an' there's my han',
  Dear Scotland, aye tae thee!

    Chorus.—My heart is Scotland's yet!

THE BONNETS O' GLENGARRY.

O' a' the hats that e'er I saw,
  The brawest ane amang them a'
Is made o' neither felt nor straw,
  The bonnets o' Glengarry!

For comfort they can ne'er be beat,
They're baith a pleasure an' a treat,
They fit the croon o' man sae neat,
  The bonnets o' Glengarry!

They stan' the test o' wind an' weather,
When buskit wi' a braw big feather,
An' twa three sprigs o' Hielan' heather,
  The bonnets o' Glengarry!

Whan Scotlan' was in sore distress,
Her sodger lads, in Hielan' dress,
Rose up in airms her cause to bless,
  Wi' bonnets o' Glengarry!

PATRIOTIC.

Whan England fought at Waterloo,
She cau'd for Scotlan's help sae true,
An' tae the front oor laddies flew,
    Wi' bonnets o' Glengarry.

Then get awa' wi' this an that,
Your "gerry," "lum" an'. "cockit hat!"
A fig for them that's sneerin' at
    My bonnet o' Glengarry!

Noo, let me say "guid-bye" to you,
An' tak' my Hielan' bonnet noo,
Nae ither clout shall croon my broo,
    Than that frae auld Glengarry!

JUBILEE SONG.

THE GOLDEN-WEDDING OF A NATION.

ALL hail to thee—VICTORIA!
   A name we all revere,
Thy loyal sons in Canada
   Send forth a British cheer;
Across the ocean's briny foam
   We hail thy Jubilee,—
Thou knowest that we love thee well,
   Thy subjects true are we.

CHORUS:

   Then sing the praise of England's Queen,
      Whose many virtues crown her station;
   O'er all the earth this day is seen
      The golden-wedding of a nation.

The sun ne'er sets on thy domains,
   Thy flag floats o'er the free;
Thy colonies, like precious gems,
   Bespangle every sea!
Thy ships of war, like buttresses,
   Defend thy honour true,
And not a son of thine would shrink
   To shed his blood for you!

      CHORUS.—Then sing the praise, etc.

PATRIOTIC.

O may thy life, our noble Queen,
　　Be spared from grief and pain,
And may the land we love so well,
　　Her prominence maintain;
For fifty years thy loving rule
　　Hath blessed us day by day;
Ah! we shall miss thee, gracious Queen,
　　When thou art called away!

Chorus·

Then sing the praise of England's Queen,
　　Whose many virtues crown her station;
O'er all the earth this day is seen
　　The golden-wedding of a nation.

YOUNG CANADA!

YOUNG Canada! Arise! Arise!
   Let Wisdom open wide your eyes.
Be lulled by neither threats nor lies,
   Stand well the test of nations!

Though others sell their birthright cheap,
   Be ours inviolate to keep
The rights and liberties we reap
   Through contact with great nations!

Be true to country, Queen, and laws,
Defend the " Statutes " clause by clause,
Stand by the right and Freedom's cause,
   A peer among the nations!

Our sires were men of noble birth,
'Mong nations foremost on the earth,
Where mountains rise, and seas engirth
   The glad homes of free nations!

PATRIOTIC.

Our heritage—from sea to sea—
A glorious home for men shall be,
As long as they shall dare be free,
    And stand among the nations!

Our boast shall be "The Maple Leaf!"
Our toil's reward—the golden sheaf!
Enough for us, and for relief
    Of other poorer nations!

We envy not our neighbour's land,
We'll guard our own with sword in hand,
And by our attitude command
    Respect from other nations.

IMRIE'S POEMS.

THE SONS OF ENGLAND.

Respectfully Dedicated to the Sons of England in Canada.

Copyrighted.   Prof. J. F. Johnstone, Toronto.

1. The sons of England are her boast, They love her as of

yore; Then pledge to her a loy - al toast, As oft we've done be -

- fore!   Her   sons are free! By   land   or sea, They

know not cra - ven fear! They dare to fight For

God and right, For home and kin - dred dear.

PATRIOTIC.

THE SONS OF ENGLAND.

RESPECTFULLY DEDICATED TO THE SONS OF ENGLAND IN CANADA.

THE sons of England are her boast,
   They love her as of yore,
Then pledge to her a loyal toast.
   As oft we've done before!

   CHORUS.—Her sons are free,
       By land or sea,
   They know not craven fear!
       They dare to fight
       For God and right,
   For home, and kindred dear!

Should foreign powers invade her strand
   And taunt her with their boasts,
Her free-born sons from many a land
   Would rally round her coasts.

   CHORUS.—" Her sons are free!"

America would send her share
   Across Atlantic's wave,
In Freedom's cause their swords declare,
   Their mother-land to save.

   CHORUS.—" Her sons are free!"

From Canada would gladly go,
　Rose, Thistle, Shamrock green!
They'd help to fight a common foe
　And shield their royal Queen.

　　CHORUS.—" Her sons are free ! "

From far across old Neptune's line
　Behold ! a loyal band,
Australia—India—would combine
　To lend a helping hand.

　　CHORUS.—" Her sons are free ! "

From distant islands of the sea
　Would rise a gallant host,
To prove that England shall be free,
　And guarded well her coast.

　　CHORUS.—" Her sons are free ! "

PATRIOTIC.

THE CANADIAN NATION.

AN ACROSTIC.

The Canadian Nation! This fair new land!
Her name shall yet among great nations stand,
Each son a link in one true loyal band!

Canadian to the core!—where prairies roll,
And northward far to the untrodden pole,
No limit East or West but boundless sea,—
All this fair land is ours!—and we are free!
Down through the ages yet to come and go
In this new land a nation strong shall grow,
And send her produce o'er the earth afar,
Nor shrink to guard her own in time of war!

Nation *from* Nations!—all of them were free!
A patriot's boast is—" BOUNDLESS FAITH IN THEE!"
The Briton and the Gaul shall brothers dwell,
In all that makes for peace seek to excel;
One name, one language, and one destiny,
No home for traitors shall be found in thee!

THE BRITISH ARMS.

THE BRITISH ARMS.

OLD England's flag floats o'er the free,—
　　The Cross, Red, White and Blue,
The British Arms, by land or sea,
　　Defends the brave and true;
Then let us sing her praises well,
　　The land we love so dear,
And of her many conquests tell,
　　Won by a British cheer!

　　　　CHORUS:
　　Hurrah! hurrah! the British Arms!
　　　　All tyrant threats defy;
　　We fear no foe, nor war's alarms,
　　　　Our motto—" Win or die!"

Old England's steel has stood the test
　　On many a foreign field,
Her sons, the noblest and the best,
　　They know not how to yield;
Her colonies, like precious gems,
　　Bespangle every sea,
Victoria's well-worn diadems
　　Shine o'er the brave and free!

　　　　CHORUS:
　　Hurrah! hurrah! the British Arms!
　　　　All tyrant threats defy;
　　We fear no foe, nor war's alarms,
　　　　Our motto—" Win or die!"

THE HIELAN' FLING.

DEDICATED TO THE GAELIC SOCIETY, TORONTO.

GAE 'wa wi' a' your fancy trash,
　　The piper to me bring !
The dances noo are wishy-wash,
　　Gie me the Hielan' fling !
It makes my bluid loup like a boy's
　　To hear the bagpipes skirl,
Baith young an' auld may weel rejoice
　　To see the kilties birl.

Bring oot yer lads an' lassies fair
　　Upon the village green,
An' let me see them dance aince mair,—
　　A sicht for auld Scotch e'en !
I feel as licht's a feather noo—
　　Ma feet 'll no 'bide still ;
I think I'll jine the lassies too,
　　An' dance wi' richt guidwill !

PATRIOTIC.

Hech! Geordie, man! that sounds fu' weel,
    Whan ye blaw up yer chanter!
I feel I maist could fecht the deil,
    An' mak' him tak' a canter!
Noo, in their place, they a' advance,
    An' beck an' bow thegither,
An' lauch to see us jine the dance—
    Their faither an' their mither!

An' what for no! I'd like to ken,
    Should we no feel sae jolly?
A turn like this ta'en noo an' then
    Is cure for melancholy!
Then blaw awa', guid Geordie, man,
    An' geist in "double time!"
A'm sure we'll dae the best we can,
    Hech! this is unco' prime!

A BUNCH O' HEATHER.

ADDRESS ON RECEIVING A BUNCH OF HIGHLAND HEATHER
IN AMERICA.

DEAR token frae my native lan',
  Thou bonnie bunch o' heather!
I'll shelter ye wi' tender han'
  Frae oor extremes o' weather;
I'll plant ye in a pat o' mool
  Brought a' the way frae Oban,
An' slochan ye wi' water cool
  An' clear as frae Loch Loman'!

An' when the Scotchman's day comes roon—
  Saint Andra's day sae cheerie—
I'll tak' ye wi' me to the toon,
  To busk my auld Glengarry;
An' you'll see faces there you ken,
  Wha speiled wi' me the heather,—
Braw Hielan' lasses an' their men
  Shall dance a reel thegither!

Then will I gie ye bit-by-bit,
    Each ano a sprig o' heather,—
To keep ye a' I'll no be fit
    Aince we meet a' thegither!
At sight o' ye we'll a' feel good,
    We loe sae ane anither;
For, ye maun ken, we're unco prood
    O' Scotlan' an' her heather!

How aft your purple face has seen
    Auld Scotia's heroes gather?
How aft the martyr's bluid hath been
    Spill'd ruthless on the heather?
For Freedom, Liberty, an' Right,
    Read Scotlan's deathless story,
Oor faithers left us by their might
    A heritage o' glory!

IMRIE'S POEMS.

CANADA!

NATIONAL ANTHEM.

Copyrighted. Music by Prof. J. F. Johnstone, Toronto.

1. Come, let us all u-nite, To sing our coun-try's praise; For God, and home, and right, Our voi-ces now we raise:—

CHORUS.

Dear Can-a-da, to thee! Home of the brave and free! With heart and voice We now re-joice, To sing in praise of thee!

PATRIOTIC.

CANADA!

NATIONAL ANTHEM.

COME, let us all unite,
 To sing our country's praise;
For God, and home, and right,
 Our voices now we raise:—
  CHORUS—
   Dear Canada, to thee,
   Home of the brave and free,
    With heart and voice
    We now rejoice
   To sing in praise of thee!

From sea to sea our land
 Extends her vast domain,
'Mid scenes sublime and grand
 We sing this glad refrain:
CHORUS—"Dear Canada to thee!" &c.

We'll welcome, with a cheer,
 Each hardy son of toil;
For happy homes are here,
 With fruitful virgin soil!
CHORUS—"Dear Canada to thee!" &c.

Let prairie, wood, and field,
 Re-echo this our song;
Our sons shall never yield,
 What rights to them belong!
CHORUS—"Dear Canada to thee!" &c.

Then wave our flag on high
 The Maple-leaf and Rose,
For Canada we'll die
 Or vanquish all her foes!
CHORUS—"Dear Canada to thee!" &c.

ON A VISIT TO THE "OLD COUNTRY."

ACROSS the wide Atlantic sea
　Our steamer speeds her way,
Great billows rolling grand and free
　Rest not by night or day.

At last the land recedes from sight,—
　The great new land of hope,
Where enterprise and honest might
　Find fair and ample scope.

A week has pass'd, yet sea and sky
　Seem all of earth to me,
Until at last the welcome cry
　Is heard with joy and glee:—

"Land, ho!—land, ho!"—a sailor cries,
　But naught to us is seen;
An hour or two, and then our eyes
　Behold the welcome scene:—

Great headlands rise, like sentries bold,
　Or guardians of the land;
Their tops, like helmets, shine with gold
　In sunset hues so grand!

Still on we speed, with hope and joy
　Our hearts feel like to sing!
Our thoughts on "home" find sweet employ
　As early scenes up-spring!

PATRIOTIC.

The fair green hills of Ireland rise,
　Resplendent to the view,
And seem an earthly Paradise
　To loving hearts and true!

'Tis hard to leave the deck to-night,
　I scarce can go to sleep;
I toss and dream, till morning light
　Comes shining o'er the deep!

Now, dear old Scotia's mountains rise
　As up the Clyde we steam,
Like friends of old they cheer our eyes,
　Or like a pleasant dream!

At last we reach the same old pier
　Where years ago we parted,
Here once we wept, now joy's glad tear
　From loving eyes has started!

Oh, friends of early days, and "home"
　Of childhood's happy years!
My thoughts are yours where'er I roam,
　For you my prayers and tears!

HAME—YET NO AT HAME!

I TOOK my way ayont the sea
  Wi' thoughts on pleasure bent,
Nigh twenty years had gane ower me
  Since frae my hame I went.

Bit noo I'm here I stranger feel
  Than if I were abroad,
I find the spots I kent sae weel
  Caw'd some new-fangled road!

I daunder up an' doon the street
  Where aince I used to play,
An' scarce a kent face dae I meet
  The lee-lang simmer's day!

My heart is sair—I canna tell
  The reason why it's sae—
An' aftentimes I ask mysel'
  Why do I feel sae wae?

I ask for Jock, an' Tam, an' Will—
  My cronies a' o' yore:
Some gane awa'—some cauld an' still—
  An' few are to the fore!

Imagination's a' at faut
  I find oot to my cost—
For Time his subtle change has wrought,
  Kent faces a' are lost!

PATRIOTIC.

I pictur'd them as when I last
    Beheld each bonnie bro',—
The lads an' lassies o' the past
    Were men an' women noo!

An' some had even quite forgot
    That ever I had been,
Until we minded o' a lot
    O' scenes we each had seen!

Then had we mony a hearty laugh
    At a'e thing an' anither,
An', as a social cup we'd quaff,
    We felt each like a brither.

We took a trip far doon the Clyde
    Amang the hills an' heather,
'Twas then I thocht I'd like to bide
    In Scotlan' a' thegither!

The hills were just the very same,
    The lochs an' glens sae bonnie,
I felt aince mair I was at hame—
    An' proud o' hame as ony.

Oh! Scotlan', thou shalt ever be
    A patriot's boast an' glory;
I'll brag o' you when ower the sea,
    An' aften tell this story!

BRUCE AND BANNOCKBURN.

IN COMMEMORATION OF JUNE 24TH, 1314.

LET Scotia's sons with honor tell
Of how our fathers fought so well,
And how proud Edward's legions fell
   Upon the field of Bannockburn !

Our sires knew well that on that day
The fate of Scotland's future lay,
Yet eager were they for the fray
   Upon the field of Bannockburn !

De Bruce reviewed his trusty band,
And o'er them stretched his brave right hand :
*"Fight for your rights and this fair land,
   Or die with me at Bannockburn !"*

The dawn of day crept o'er the hill,
The Scottish army—calm and still—
Committed to God's holy will
   The loss or gain of Bannockburn !

PATRIOTIC.

On ! on ! the English forces flew,
A hundred men to one I trew,
Yet routed were they by a few
    Brave Scottish Clans at Bannockburn !

Ere yet that evening's sun had set
The field with English blood was wet,
For there the Sons of Scotland met
    To claim their rights at Bannockburn !

Let sires their sons this history tell
Of how our fathers fought and fell,
For Freedom that they loved so well
    And won for us at Bannockburn !

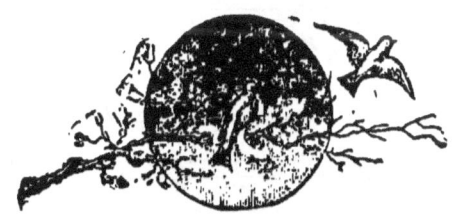

PATRIOTIC.

SCOTCH DAINTIES.

GIE a Scotchman a guid cog o' brose,
   Wi' milk just new drawn frae the coo',
Feth ye'll no see him turn up his nose,
   But tak' them, an' then smack his moo'!

CHORUS:
   Brose, parritch, kail, haggis an' bannocks,
     Are dainties abune a' compare!
   Nae English, French, Yankees or Canucks,
     Could mak' such a gran' bill o' fare!

Guid parritch for weans is sae healthy,
   It mak's them grow strong, fat an' weel,
Dyspeptics are aye 'mang the wealthy,—
   They eat what wad sicken an eel!

     CHORUS.—"Brose, parritch, kail," &c.

Noo, what is sae guid as Scotch kail,
   Wi' carrots, an' turnips, an' leeks;
Hielan'men are braw, hearty an' hale—
   Yet gang a' the year without breeks!

     CHORUS.—"Brose, parritch, kail," &c.

But the haggis is king o' the table,—
   A Scotchman's maist toothfu' delight,
By dining on that he is able
   To match ony twa in a fight!

     CHORUS.—"Brose, parritch, kail," &c.

PATRIOTIC.

When spying for game in Glen Sannox,
    Ahint a wheen stanes on my knees,
What's sweeter than crumpin' oat bannocks,
    An' eating a' whang o' guid cheese?
          CHORUS.—" Brose, parritch, kail," &c.

Brose, parritch, kail, haggis an' bannocks
    Wad mak' lean consumptives grow fat,
Though they'd sleep oot at nicht in hammocks,
    They'd ne'er be a bit waur o' that!
          CHORUS.—" Brose, parritch, kail," &c.

Then gie us oor dainty Scotch farin',
    We'll honour the auld muckle pat!
For pastry an' pies we're no carin',
    Scotch laddies are no built wi' that!
          CHORUS:
    Brose, parritch, kail, haggis an' bannocks,
        Are dainties abune a' compare!
    Nae English, French, Yankees or Canucks,
        Could mak' such a gran' bill o' fare!

LOVE, HOME, AND FRIENDSHIP.

Love, Home and Friendship.

WHERE DOTH BEAUTY DWELL?

LOOK for the first faint streaks of morn
   That gild the eastern sky,
Another day in beauty born,
   As mounts the sun on high;
Tinting the tops of highest towers
   With crimson and with gold,
Melting the dew-drops from the flowers
   That peepingly unfold:
There doth "the beautiful" abide
   In calm security;
The rosy morn—deck'd like a bride—
   Of virgin purity!

Look for the eyes that beam with love,
   And sparkle with delight,
To meet thy gaze—like stars above—
   Brightest in thy dark night;
Dispelling every thought of sin
   From out thy heart's great deep,
Chasing the darkness from within,
   Or soothe thy fears to sleep:
There doth "the beautiful" abide
   In full maturity;
And there may thy fond heart reside
   Through all futurity!

HEART QUESTIONINGS.

WHAT stirs an emotion
As deep as the ocean,
And strong as the hills that tower above?
'Tis the sound of a sigh,
As the zephyrs go by,
That tells in a breath the presence of Love!

What is seen in the glance,
As true lovers advance,
That kindles a flame which never can die?
'Tis a spark from above,
From the altar of Love,
Dropp'd unerringly down from on high!

As the loving hands clasp,
What is told in the grasp
That quickens the pulse and glows on the cheek?
'Tis "the story of old,"
In that loving enfold,
The language of Love that words cannot speak!

Whence the tones that can thrill,
Without effort or will,
And woo the heart's fond admiration?
They are notes from the choir,
With the golden lyre,
Tuned by Love's sublime inspiration!

LOVE, HOME, AND FRIENDSHIP.

    Oh! from whence comes the bliss
    Of love's first fervent kiss,
That rapturous outflow of feeling?
    'Tis a faint echo given
    Of earth's foretaste of Heaven,
By fond hearts their fulness revealing!

    Whence the breathings of soul
    That defies our control,
Those sweet communings of heart with heart?
    'Tis a gift from above,
    'Tis the token of love,
Once possesss'd, time or death cannot part!

THE STAR OF LOVE.

IS Love a star?
Yes, 'tis a star
Of heav'nly magnitude afar;
In darkest night
The purest light,
No baneful doubt should ever mar.

It is a star—
The Polar star—
That guides the sailor on the sea,
Where'er he roam,
To love and home,
Across the boundless ocean free.

Storms may arise
In life's pure skies,
And gathering clouds bedim our day;
But Love's bright eye,
Like star in sky,
Will seek to guide us on our way!

Love reigns supreme,
An endless theme,
Love rules the world with gentle hand;
As captives, we
Desire to be
Encircl'd with her golden band!

A BOUQUET OF FLOWERS.

THE present you send,
My dear loving friend—
A beautiful bouquet of flowers,—
　　Is precious to me,
　　As coming from thee,
With perfume of bright sunny bowers.

　　It reminds me of home,
　　Where once we did roam,
'Mid flow'rs in the garden at play;
　　As swift pass'd the hours
　　In Flora's sweet bowers,
And short seem'd the summer's long day.

　　But life, like the flowers,
　　Hath changeable hours,
And sunshine and show'r intervene;
　　Yet love in the heart
　　Can beauty impart,
And help to make life "evergreen."

　　Let friendship and truth
　　Encompass our youth,
From sorrow and trouble 'twill save;
　　In sweetest content
　　Our lives shall be spent,
And flow'rs strew our path to the grave!

TRUE LOVE.

'TIS a magic spell,
Which lovers know well,
In sunshine and shower the same;
Ever old, yet new,
Both constant and true,
And seeks neither self nor fame.

Unheard or confest,
As seemeth it best,
Its tale it may never unfold;
Yet all know the pow'r
Of Love's happy hour,
Its memory never grows old!

'Tis a golden key,
Be it sigh or plea,
That opens the door of the heart;
And treasures untold
Doth ever unfold,
Which riches could never impart.

Then cherish with care
A jewel so rare,
And dim not its lustre with scorn;
'Twill lighten the gloom
From cradle to tomb,
And heal the heart bleeding and torn.

Love never can die,
Its home is on high,
And God will yet claim what He gives;
And love He hath giv'n,
To make earth a heav'n,
True love in the heart ever lives!

LOVE AND CHARITY.

OH! for sweet and tender Love,
    Pure and faithful ever,
Wooing like the gentle dove,
    Flowing as a river!
Smiles, like flowers, adorn her path,
    Peaceful—soul-refreshing,
Freely giving all she hath,
    Earth's most potent blessing!

Love and Charity are one—
    Not of earth's conceiving,
To possess is heaven begun,
    Toil and care relieving;
Let Love lead us hand-in-hand
    A-down the misty years,
Guiding to the better land—
    Where God shall wipe all tears.

THE HUMBER "FAIRY."

THE HUMBER "FAIRY."

Heard ye of the Humber "Fairy"?
Know ye that her name is Mary?
Queen of beauty—light, and airy,
    Winsome, yet so shy;
In a cottage by the river,
Where the ferns nod and quiver,
There my fancy turneth ever,
    For her smile I sigh!

When the sun is slowly setting,
Then, my heart with fulness fretting,
All but love of her forgetting,
    To my skiff I hie;
Off to "my Fairy-land" I glide,
Each feather'd oar on either side
Like Cupid's wings, they skim the tide—
    O'er the waters fly!

O'er the Bay the moon is stealing,
All her loveliness revealing,
Then to each fond heart appealing,
    Love looks eye to eye!
Glide we up the Humber river,
Where the rushes sigh and quiver,
Plight our love to each for ever,—
    Love that will not die!

A SOUVENIR OF LOVE.

Tenderly. (Copyrighted.) Music by E. Gledhill.

Dearest, sweetest, fondest, best, Lean your head up-on my breast;

Lov-ing arms shall thee entwine, Loving hands be placed in mine;

Throbbing hearts with pleasure beat, Happy eyes in gladness meet;

Peace and joy now reign supreme, Love our all absorbing theme....

Dearest, sweetest, fondest, best, Lean your head up-on my breast;

Lov-ing arms shall thee en-twine, Loving hands be placed in mine.

A SOUVENIR OF LOVE.

DEAREST, sweetest, fondest, best,
Lean your head upon my breast;
Loving arms shall thee entwine,
Loving hands be placed in mine;
Throbbing hearts with pleasure beat,
Happy eyes in gladness meet;
Peace and joy now reign supreme,
Love our all-absorbing theme.

Picture of a living love,
True as angel-notes above;
Constant as the Polar star
Shining in the heavens afar;
Deep and boundless as the sea,
Ever pure and ever free;
Warm and bright as Southern skies,
Earthly Eden—Paradise!

Love like this doth ever sing,
Echoes wake and echoes ring;
Love and pain *may* sometimes meet,
Love can make the pain a sweet;
Grief and care shall flee away,
Darkest night be turn'd to day,
Winter snows to Summer showers,
Autumn leaves to Spring's fresh flowers.

Sordid pleasures have their day,
Truth and Love shall ne'er decay;
Heaven and earth their blessings give,
Love and Truth shall ever live.
Then, let Love our bosoms thrill,
Empty hearts may have their fill;
The poorest may be rich in love,
Bless'd on earth and crown'd above!

EMBLEMS OF FRIENDSHIP.

FRIENDSHIP is a GOLDEN BAND
　　Linking life with life,
Heart to heart, and hand to hand,
　　Antidote to strife.

Friendship is a SILKEN CORD
　　Beautiful and strong,
Guarding, by each kindly word,
　　Loving hearts from wrong.

Friendship is a BEACON-LIGHT
　　On life's rocky shore,
Brightest in our darkest night
　　When the breakers roar.

Friendship is an IRON SHIELD
　　Where life's cruel darts
Ever may be forced to yield
　　Ere they wound true hearts.

Friendship is the GIFT OF GOD
　　Freely to us given,
As the flowers that gem the sod,
　　Or the light of heaven!

EYES THAT SPEAK.

Copyrighted.   Music by Prof. J. F. Johnstone, Toronto.

1. Give me the eyes that speak of Love, And spar-kle in their

glad · · ness,   Like twinkling orbs   of light a - bove;

Dispelling care and sad-ness, Dispelling care.... and sad-ness.

Which makes this earth a Par-a-dise, Tho' hum-ble be our

dwelling; And causing thoughts of love to rise From hearts with fulness

welling, And causing thoughts of love to rise From hearts with fulness welling.

LOVE, HOME, AND FRIENDSHIP.

EYES THAT SPEAK.

GIVE me the eyes that speak of Love,
    And sparkle in their gladness,
Like twinkling orbs of light above,
    Dispelling care and sadness;
Which make this earth a Paradise,
    Though humble be our dwelling,
And causing thoughts of love to rise
    From hearts with fulness welling.

Give me the eyes whose tears of Grief
    Are shed for our condoling,
Whose sympathy is sure relief
    To hearts that need consoling;
More precious than the jewel rare
    That glistens in its setting,
Are eyes that speak the love they bear,
    All selfishness forgetting.

Give me the eyes that speak of Peace
    And shed a halo o'er us,
Whose beams can cause all strife to cease,
    And tune our hearts in chorus
To sing in unison the strain
    Which God hath set before us:
"Let peace on earth for ever reign,"—
    Hark! angels join the chorus!

Give me the eyes of Faith to see,
　Behind the clouds of sorrow,
My Father's hand still guiding me
　On to the bright to-morrow;
And onward still, through good and ill,
　His eye shall safely guide me;
All dangers past, safe home at last,
　With Jesus close beside me!

WHAT CAN LOVE DO?

LOVE can make the eyes shine bright,
Love can brighten darkest night;
Love can make the lover gush,
Love can make the maiden blush.

Love can warm the coldest heart,
Love can kindest words impart;
Love can happiness bestow,
Love can never answer " No."

Love can sing the gayest song,
Love can make the weak feel strong;
Love can lighten every care,
Love can sweetly trials bear.

Love can sit enthron'd in state,
Love can rule a nation great;
Love can noble laws impart,
Love can win the people's heart.

Love can educate the mind,
Love can aye be true and kind;
Love can greatest pleasure give,
Love can teach us how to live.

Love can sweetest comfort bring,
Love can take from Death the sting;
Love can greatest burdens bear,
Love can all our sorrows share.

If our lives are pure and free,
Love must then our teacher be;
Daily learn the heavenly plan:—
"Love to God and love to man."

LOVE'S PROGRESS.

WE met, but not as strangers meet,
In busy mart, or crowded street,—
No hurried glance could well suffice
To meet the gaze of Love's surprise;
That look a "tale of old" reveal'd,
Which would not, could not, be conceal'd,
And well bespoke love's sweet content,
Though speechless on our way we went.

Again we met—not like the past,—
The spell of Love had now been cast;
Still, words refused to tell the tale
Which redden'd cheeks that erst were pale,
And fluttered hearts with new-born joy,
And gave our thoughts such sweet employ;
We smiled, and often met to smile,
And thus did Love our hearts beguile.

At last I spoke, in hope and fear,
A few short words, deep, true, sincere;
Then love in transport met the gaze
Of love return'd 'mid glad amaze;
Her stammering tones, and modest start,
Answered the gladness in my heart;
I kissed joy's tear from off her face,
And clasp'd her in my warm embrace.

We loved, and love still dwells secure,
And shall while life and love endure;
Our love is sweet, and all is well,
For in each other's hearts we dwell;
Like streams which meet and onward glide,
Till lost in ocean's boundless tide,
We two have met no more to part,
For Love hath join'd us heart to heart!

LOVE-LINKS.

THE LOOK of a loving eye
    Tells all it knows,
    Like blushing rose,
And lives to be lov'd—or die!

The TOUCH of a gentle hand
    A tale doth tell
    Love knoweth well
And only Love understand.

The TONES of a loving voice,
    Like birds in Spring,
    Doth sweetly sing,
And maketh the heart rejoice!

The JOY of a love-lit heart
    No tongue can tell:
    Its potent spell
Neither time nor distance part!

Sweet words that can never die;
    "Wilt thou be mine?"
    "I WILL BE THINE!"
Is the maiden's faint reply.

These LINKS must not be broken,
    Oh! no! no! no!
    But stronger grow,
Love's changeless, deathless token!

THE FLOWER OF THE FAMILY.

THE Angel of Death came hovering near,
   To kiss the fair cheek of a child ;
He left a dark shadow of hope and fear,
   And a mother's heart throbbing wild.
A fond father knelt, with a trembling heart,
   By the couch where his treasure lay ;
Though he tried to smile, yet the tears would start,
   While he vainly brush'd them away.

The silence of death was broken at last,
   By sobs of a mother's first grief,
As the eyes of her boy to hers were cast,
   With appealing looks for relief ;
The father's strong arms encircl'd the child,
   And sooth'd him at last to his rest,
While he clos'd his eyes and lovingly smil'd,
   As he winged his way to the blest !

A prayer for submission and faith was sent
   To the God of all love and grace ;
And a ray of light in the dark was lent
   From their heavenly Father's face,
As He taught them to lift their hearts above
   The flower which to them was given ;
While He would transplant, with infinite love,
   That flower in the garden of Heaven !

LOVE, HOME, AND FRIENDSHIP.

ROMPING WITH THE CHILDREN.

MIMIC battle,
Din and rattle,
Romping with the children after tea;
How they giggle,
Laugh and wriggle,
Crowing as they triumph over me!

"Make him a horse,"
That's "Pa," of course,
They, the merry riders full of glee;
Though not much ground,
Yet round and round,
Till they drive the wind right out of me!

At last content,
And I near spent,
Loudly they call for "a song" from me!
I laugh and grin,
And then begin,
Hugging a little one on each knee!

"So here goes, Papa,
And one from Mamma,
And another when you can come home;
Just answer me this,
Is it nice to kiss
When you want through the dear telefome?"

"Hello?" I replied,
With fatherly pride,
"I've got them as snug as can be;
I'll give them all back,
With many a smack,
As soon as I come home to tea!"

"OUR JOHNNIE."*

WE hae had a happy time,
    Since hame cam Johnnie;
Wi' a face like angel sweet,
Stealin' a' o'or kisses neat,
Creepin' roun on hauns an' feet,
    Was o'or wee Johnnie!

Langest day maun hae its close,
    Alas! puir Johnnie;
Death cam in sae grim an' cauld,
Chill'd the lammie in the fauld,
Ta'en the young and left the auld,
    Puir deed wee Johnnie.

Ta'en awa' in life's spring time,
    O'or ain dear Johnnie;
Mither's heart in anguish wild,
Faither grudges sair his child,
Yet tae God baith reconcil'd;
    We'll gang tae Johnnie.

---

* Lines written on seeing the above epitaph on a tombstone over a little grave in Mount Pleasant Cemetery, Toronto, erected in affectionate remembrance of John McKinnon, born Oct. 7, 1874; died Jan. 31, 1881.

Ainst the light o' a' o'or house,
    O'or ain wee Johnnie;
Noo the light is ta'en awa'
Darkness seems tae cover a',
Nane can comfort us ava
    Bit o'or wee Johnnie!

'Neath the souchan willow tree
    Lies o'or wee Johnnie;
Just beneath a hillock green,
Whaur the daisies may be seen,
Wi' the buttercups between,
    Sleeps o'or wee Johnnie.

Aft we shed the bitter tear
    For o'or wee Johnnie;
Then look up wi' faith abuin,
Whaur nae sorrow creepeth in,
There, secure frae death an' sin,
    Bides o'or wee Johnnie!

"PAPA'S PET."

DOWN a crowded thoroughfare
 Walk'd a little stranger,
Light blue eyes and golden hair,
 Scarcely knew her danger!

Gaily dress'd, so clean and neat,
 Ribbons without measure!
Stockings white and slipper'd feet,
 Some one's darling treasure!

Heedless pass'd the crowd along,—
 Business hours are pressing,
None in all that busy throng
 Stopp'd to make caressing!

Now and then an anxious look
 O'er her face came stealing,
Wise as any sage's book,
 Troubled heart revealing!

Looking for her mother's smile
 In that sea of faces;
None her fears could there beguile,
 Wearily she paces!

See! the blue eyes fill with tears,
 And her bosom, heaving,
Shows the crowd her anxious fears
 Need some kind relieving!

Soon a kindly stranger came,
    And wip'd the cheeks so wet:—
"Tell me, Sissy, what's your name?"
    "My papa calls me '*Pet!*'"

Here the stranger dropt a sigh,—
    A sigh of sad regret;
One he claim'd above the sky,
    Ah! once he call'd her "*Pet!*"

How he kiss'd that little child,
    Kiss'd all her tears away;
Till at last she sweetly smil'd,
    Just like a summer's day!

Soon he found her father's home,
    Kept chatting all the way;
Never more from thence to roam
    Until her wedding day!

"PAPA'S PET."

Music by Rev. J. B. Dykes, Mus. Doc.

1. Down a crowd-ed thor-ough-fare,

Walk'd a lit-tle strang - - - er;

Light blue eyes and gold-en hair, ...

Scarce-ly knew her dan - - ger!

IMRIE'S POEMS.

A KISS THROUGH THE TELEPHONE.

A KISS THROUGH THE TELEPHONE.

THE telephone,
   In merry tone,
Rang " Tinkelty-tinkelty-tink !"
   I put my ear
   Close up to hear,
And what did I hear, do you think ?

   " Papa, hello !
   'Tis me you know ! "
The voice of my own little Miss ;
   " You went away
   From home to-day,
But you never gave me—a kiss !

   " It was a mistake,
   I was not awake,
Before you went out of the house ;
   I think that a kiss
   Will not be amiss
If I give it—sly as a mouse !

"So here goes, Papa,
    And one for Mamma,
And another when you can come home :
    Just answer me this,
    Is it nice to kiss
When you want through the dear telefome?"

"Hello?" I replied,
    With fatherly pride,
"I've got them as snug as can be ;
    I'll give them all back,
    With many a smack,
As soon as I come home to tea !"

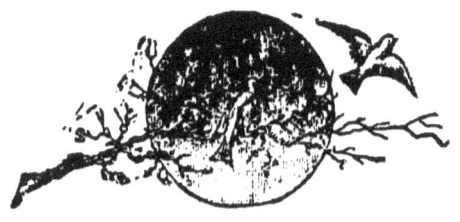

A KISS THROUGH THE TELEPHONE.

"Papa, hello!
'Tis me, you know!"
The voice of my own little Miss;
"You went away
From home to-day,
But you never gave me—a kiss!"

THE LOVER'S IDEAL.

I KNOW a face—a lovely face,
  'Tis imag'd on my heart,
Whose form is one of matchless grace,
  From her I'll never part.

I know a voice of sweetest tone,
  That speaks in accents low,
Yet has a power all its own
  To make my heart o'erflow.

I know a place where lovers meet,
  There Nature reigns supreme,
'Tis there we hold our converse sweet,
  Love is our only theme.

I know a heart whose depth of love
  Time, life, nor death can measure,
Next to my hope of bliss above
  I value this dear treasure.

I heard a vow—a solemn vow,
  'Twas register'd in heaven :
That all our future life from now
  Shall to our love be given.

I know a home—a happy home,
  By love 'tis daily lighted,
Where kindred hearts ne'er seek to roam
  Since by their vows united !

THE BABY'S PORTRAIT.

STEADY now, young "Chatterbox!"
Rosy cheeks and raven locks;
Mamma wants your portrait now,
Smile again and smooth your brow!
Touch your mouth with finger-tips,
Pearly teeth and ruby lips;
Papa's pride and mamma's pet,
High upon a cushion set!

Rolling eyes of azure blue,
Watching, wondering, "what's-a-do!"
While the artist smiles and grins,
Ere he to his task begins.
Steady now, young "Chatterbox!"
Sly as any little fox;—
Tinkling bells—the signal given—
"One, two, three, four, five, six, seven!"

For a minute silence reigns,
Pleasure leaps in all our veins,
Baby's picture's now complete,
Lifelike, true, and oh, so sweet!
Every one is positive
Never was such negative;
Beauty smiles at beauty's self,
Each one hugs the little elf!

Soon a dainty frame is made,
In the frame the portrait laid,
Where it lay for many a day,
As the years roll'd swift away ;
Oft the mother look'd and smil'd
At the picture of her child,
Now a happy, blushing bride,
Still her father's joy and pride !

But at last there came a day
When the bride must pass away,
Claim'd by lover of her own,
Happy in that love alone ;
And, 'mong presents rich and rare,
One was prized—a portrait fair—
Smiling as in days of yore,
Now a "Chatterbox" no more !

LEARNING "THE TWINS" TO WALK.

TWO little "Toddlekins" learning to walk,
   Mamma and sister supporting;
Trying to toddle, and learning to talk,
   'Mid chatting, laughing, and sporting!

Mamma seems proud of her two little pets,
   Johnnie and Winnie she calls them;
Dolly consumes all the kisses she gets,—
   No "Dolly" could thrive without them!

One little—two little—three little steps!
   Cautiously, carefully tended;
Mamma's strong arms most lovingly "keps"
   Both when "the trial" is ended!

Laughing, and crowing, and kissing all 'round,
   Everyone happy and cheerful;
A hug and a squeeze, a skip and a bound,
   A din that's perfectly fearful!

Happy the home with the children around,
   Despite all their din and rattle;
No likelier spot on earth can be found
   To nerve us for life's stern battle!

MISUNDERSTOOD!

WHAT inward pain we sometimes feel
   When we have been misunderstood,
How doth affection's warmth congeal
   When ill intent's coin'd out of good?
How many bleeding hearts there are
   Whose greatest bliss was doing good,
Yet for their love receiv'd a scar
   From dearest friend—MISUNDERSTOOD!

When death hath clos'd the eyes of one
   Whose heart beat ever for our good,
How sad to know their setting sun
   Was dimm'd by us—MISUNDERSTOOD!
'Tis then we feel the pain we gave
   A parent, friend, or neighbor good,
And grief o'erwhelms us like a wave,—
   Too late! too late!—MISUNDERSTOOD!

Oh! could we but live o'er the past,
    And weave our web of life once more,
Glad rays of sunshine would we cast
    Where doubt and darkness reign'd before!
Hope is not dead!—the Present lives!—
    Let us redeem it as we should;
The flower that's crush'd more fragrance gives
    Than had it lived—MISUNDERSTOOD!

But One there is who never fails
    To read the heart of man aright,
Though toss'd on life's tempestuous gales,
    God will sustain us by His might!
Let all our aims in life be pure—
    Men may mis-judge—still cling to good;
At last the victory shall be sure,
    And we shall then be—UNDERSTOOD!

"OUR BABY!"

CHUBBY face,
Full of grace,
Comic little glances;
Glad surprise,
Roguish eyes,
Making sweet advances!

Rosy feet,
Small and neat,
With dainty little toes;
Snug and warm,
Safe from harm,
Done up in fancy hoso!

Gaily drest,
In her best,
Just like a fairy queen;
Tiny hands,
Satin bands,
We're proud of her, I ween!

Kick and crow,
Stretch and grow,
Seems bigger every day;
Not a care
Nestles there,
But angel-smiles alway!

God above,
Full of love,
Sent this little stranger;
Now we pray,
Every day,
Shield her from all danger!

THE MOTHERLESS CHILD.

"OH! Papa, where is Ma to-day?
   I've looked in every bed!
They tell me 'Ma has gone away,'
   Aunt says that ' Ma is dead.'
I thought that she would soon be well,
   I kiss'd her yesterday;
Now where she is I cannot tell,
   I feel too sad to play."

The father, stooping, kiss'd his child,
   And strok'd her golden hair;
He strove to hide the anguish wild
   That struggl'd with despair.
The blue eyes scann'd him o'er and o'er,
   And seem'd to read him through:
"Papa, will Mamma come no more,
   And has she left you too?"

Like arrow sharp from quivering bow,
   The question smote him sore;
And grief, like ocean's ebb and flow,
   Found vent in tears once more.
He clasp'd his darling to his breast,
   Which seemed to ease his pain:
"God called your Ma; His will is best;
   We'll meet with her again!"

He carried her with tender care
  To where the coffin lay,
To view the mother, young and fair,
  Now lifeless as the clay.
" Oh! Mamma, dear! I'm here! I'm here!
  My Papa is here too!"
And on the dead there dropt a tear
  From out those eyes of blue!

Kind friends looked in and view'd a scene
  Which "touched their hearts," they said,
Then tenderly they came between
  The living and the dead.
Weep not for those whom God has ta'en
  To realms of endless light,
Our loss is their eternal gain—
  God doeth all things right.

A GOLDEN WEDDING.

FIFTY years of wedded life,
  Half a century of bliss,
Since we first were man and wife,
  What a consummation this!

Through the sunshine and the shower,
  Bound by golden bands in one,
Hand-in-hand in darkest hour,
  We the race of life have run.

True to vows of early years,
  Faithful to each other's love,
Yet with tenderness and tears,
  Ripening for the courts above.

Years of joy, and love, and peace,
  Full of happiness and trust;
Learning, as the years increase,
  God is ever wise and just.

Soon at last His voice will call
  One or other hence away;
Still remaining ONE through all,
  WEDDED THROUGH ETERNITY!

TO MY FRIENDS.

RIENDS of my earliest days and years,
Ye who dispell'd my infant fears,
And o'er me spent your prayers and tears,
    Father, Mother;
And let me pay a tribute meet
To those who watch'd my infant feet,
And shower'd on me their kisses sweet,
    Sister, Brother.

Friends of my school-days or of play,
When all was joyous, bright, and gay,
Companions dear of life's spring-day,
    Again we meet;
As memory paints the scenes anew,
In colours of the brightest hue,
When life was good, and pure, and true,
    And friendship sweet.

Friends of those years when hopes were high,
And hearts beat true, and love was nigh,
And echoes woke which ne'er shall die,
    But echoes give;
While fleeting years roll on apace,
Within my heart there is a place
That bears the likeness of each face,
    And thoughts that live!

Friends dead and gone—friends far and near—
Friends tried and true—friends ever dear,
Though sunder'd far, yet all are here,
    Close to my heart ;
And all along life's rugged way
The smile of friendship crowns the day,
And hearts are young though heads be grey :—
    Friends never part !

LOVE, HOME, AND FRIENDSHIP.

A TRIBUTE TO MOTHER.

OH, mother, dear! what memories sweet
    Call back the scenes of early years,
When thou didst tend our infant feet,
    And guard our life with pray'rs and tears.

Our little griefs, at school or play,
    We pour'd into thy willing ear;
But thou didst kiss the tears away,
    And quick dispell'd our every fear.

And, when in wilful ways we trod,
    Alas! for us, too willing feet,
Thy love did bring us back to God,
    And led us to the mercy-seat.

Thy look was love—thy smile was joy—
    Thy tears the eloquence of grief;
Thy loving voice found sweet employ
    In whisp'ring to our heart's relief.

Oh! mother dear! how much we owe
    To thee, for all thy loving care;
While memory lasts our thoughts shall go
    Back to the days of love and pray'r.

Though on this earth no more we meet,
    And surging seas between us roll,
We yet shall meet at Jesus' feet,
    Where love eternal fills the soul!

I MISS A DEAR FACE.

Music by Ernest E. Leigh, Cobourg, Ont.

1. I miss a dear face From its wont-ed place, And my heart is full of sad-ness; But look-ing a-bove To the God of love, The sor-row is chang'd to glad-ness. Ah! I know that there, In that purer air—The home of our heavenly Father—Is the one I miss, In that land of bliss, Where the an-gels love to gather.

REFRAIN. *Joyfully.*

Oh! we yet shall meet On that gold-en street, Oh! nev-er a-gain to sev-er; Earth's troubles all past, In our home at last, With ful-ness of joy for ev-er!

I MISS A DEAR FACE.

I MISS a dear face
From its wonted place,
And my heart is full of sadness;
But looking above
To the God of love,
The sorrow is chang'd to gladness.

REFRAIN—
Oh! we yet shall meet
On that golden street,
Oh! never again to sever;
Earth's troubles all past,
In our home at last,
With fulness of joy for ever!

Ah! I know that there,
In that purer air—
The home of our heavenly Father—
Is the one I miss,
In that land of bliss,
Where the angels love to gather.
REFRAIN—" Oh! we yet shall meet," etc.

A dear voice that cheers,
Through the silent years,
Is heard with its sweet, soft pleading;
And a hand that guides
Through earth's stormy tides
Hath mine in its kindly leading.
REFRAIN—" Oh! we yet shall meet," etc.

I will not repine
But daily incline
The path of my lov'd to follow;
Then, let the years pass,
Like sands in a glass,
Or sighing winds o'er the hollow!
REFRAIN—" Oh! we yet shall meet," etc.

A HUSBAND'S BIRTHDAY GREETING.

DARLING, awake! and let the sweet, glad light,
Fill eyes that love hath made so pure and bright;
So calm and deeply true, so free from guile,
So winning in their artless love-lit smile,
That I would fain obey their least behest,
And clasp thee fondly to my throbbing breast,
And tell, with untold kisses, sweetest dear,
That thou hast entered on another year!

How sweet the memory of the blissful past,
When o'er our paths love's glad spring-flowers were
    cast,
As fresh and pure as when in Eden's bowers
The first fond pair spent earth's creative hours;
Yet, dear, 'twas but the dawn of brighter days,
Such as we now enjoy, 'mid grateful praise
To Him who crowns our years with peace and love,
A sweet fore-taste of purer joys above!

Ah! clinging dear! the ivy and the oak
Are not more near when thou dost thus provoke
To deeds and words of love that plainly tell
That Love is king, and all he doth is well;
The hot tears flow, but not because of grief,
'Tis heartfelt joy which thus must find relief;
And mutely eloquent each throbbing heart
Proclaims the other as its counterpart!

LOVE, HOME, AND FRIENDSHIP.

God bless our love, for He alone can bind
In perfect union, both of heart and mind,
All those who seek in Him their source of bliss,
Of love and joy, of peace and happiness.
Oh, may thy future bright and joyful be,
From every sorrow may thy lot be free,
And through life's journey to the very end
Heaven's choicest blessings all thy way attend!

A WIFE'S LAST GOOD-BYE.

OH, husband dear, though now we part,
  And I must cross the river,
I fain would cheer thy lonely heart—
  We do not part for ever!
I go to brighter, holier ground,
  Where friendships are not hollow,
Where peace and love are ever found,
  And thou wilt surely follow.

Oh, brightly beams that happy land
  Of light, and love, and gladness,
Where we shall stand, at God's right hand,
  Free from all care and sadness.
Let faith foresee with hopeful eyes,
  That even now may borrow
A cheering ray from brighter skies
  To dissipate thy sorrow.

Oh, husband dearest, fondest, best,
  To whom my love was given,
In Jesus' love find sweetest rest,
  We'll wait for thee in Heaven;
Death cannot enter there, my love,
  Nor tears bedim the sight;
An endless love is ours above,
  With angels ever bright.

One child is safe with me in Heaven,
  The other left with you,
May wisdom from above be given
  To make him kind and true;
And when at last we four shall meet,
  Beyond the surging river,
We'll lay our crowns at Jesus' feet,
  And praise His love for ever!

MOTHER'S VOICE.

Music by Prof. J. F. Johnstone, Toronto.

1. Oh! the sound of mother's voice, 'Twas like music to my ear,

Oft it made my heart re-joice, Oft dis-pelled my anx-ious

fear; But, 'tis hush'd in si-lence now, And of grief I've

had my fill, Her last kiss up-on my brow Seems to leave its

CHORUS.

im-press still. Oh! the sound of moth-er's voice, As it ech-oes

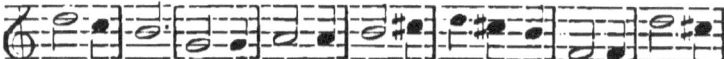

through the years, How it makes my heart rejoice, Though it melts my eyes to

tears! While I live I'll ne'er for-get Tones so full of ten-der

Rit.

love; Moth-er, dear, I'll meet thee yet, In our heavenly home a-bove!

MOTHER'S VOICE.

OH! the sound of mother's voice,
   'Twas like music to my ear,
Oft it made my heart rejoice,
   Oft dispell'd my anxious fear;
But, 'tis hush'd in silence now,
   And of grief I've had my fill,
Her last kiss upon my brow
   Seems to leave its impress still!

CHORUS—
    Oh! the sound of mother's voice,
      As it echoes through the years,
    How it makes my heart rejoice,
      Though it melts my eyes to tears!
    While I live I'll ne'er forget
      Tones so full of tender love;
    Mother, dear, I'll meet thee yet
      In our heavenly home above!

Mother's voice! I hear it still,
   Seems to come from heaven above,
Keeping back my froward will,
   Full of tenderness and love;
In my dreams I oft recall
   Each kind look of love and joy,
Now, I understand it all—
   How a mother loves her boy!

CHORUS—
    "Oh! the sound of mother's voice," &c.

Oh! the sound of mother's voice
　Are the sweetest notes of earth,
There is nothing half so choice,
　Full of love, and hope, and mirth;
Though to Heaven she has gone,
　Yet the wealth of love she gave
Hath a power to cheer me on
　From the cradle to the grave!

CHORUS—

Oh! the sound of mother's voice
　As it echoes through the years,
How it makes my heart rejoice,
　Though it melts my eyes to tears!
While I live I'll ne'er forget
　Tones so full of tender love,
Mother, dear, I'll meet thee yet
　In our heavenly home above!

CROSS'D LOVE.

A VISION cross'd my path one day,
    'Twas like a dream of pleasure,
And left a halo 'long life's way,
    For memory to treasure!
Cross'd love can live a life of hope,
    Nor all life's ills can kill it,
Though Love be blind, yet he can grope
    If fate doth only will it!

Time smoothes the furrows of our grief,
    And Patience grows with sorrow,
The future brings a sure relief,
    Let Care wait till—to-morrow!
Smile!—though thy heart be full of pain,
    There's nothing gain'd by grieving,
A vision yet will come again,
    All former ills relieving.

The rose that's left upon a tree
    May be a thing of beauty;
But, oh! the Rose that pleaseth me
    Counts sacrifice a duty!
When Love, and Truth, and Honour binds,
    Fond hearts have their fulfilling,
No life is perfect till it finds
    Its wealth of love distilling!

THE TENDER PASSION.

ERE Love had set my heart on fire,
And tuned me to devotion,
I could the fairest face admire
Without the least emotion:
 I felt as free
 As wind or sea,
Each day was full of gladness;
 But when at last
 Love's die was cast,
My joy was ting'd with sadness!

For only when my love was near
I felt the sun was shining,
Love's presence is a foe to fear
When hearts are intertwining!
 A world of bliss
 Was in each kiss,
They set our hearts a-singing;
 When call'd to part
 Sad was each heart,
True lover's fears up-bringing!

At last to ease my heart's deep pain
  I made a fair confession,
And kiss'd her o'er and o'er again,—
  Reward for Love's concession:
    We now are one
    Still shines the sun!—
All earth is full of beauty!
    Though Love be blind
    She's wondrous kind
And mindful of her duty ¡

BETROTHED.

AN ALLEGORY.

TWO lofty mountains soar'd o'erhead,
    Each side a vale of vast extent,
They knew each other well, 'twas said,
    With hoary age their forms were bent!

They guarded well that lovely vale,
    And watched, as with a mother's pride,
Two silver streams that swept the dale,
    Yet had their source on either side.

On, on they sped, like friends at play,—
    Now almost caught, now far apart;
Till—ha! ha! ha!—they lost their way,
    And join'd themselves no more to part!

The mountains smiled, and clapped their hands,
    And wished the lovers happy day!
The setting sun lent golden bands,
    The moon threw silver o'er their way!

Wide, wide, they spread their pebbly bed,
    United now were they for ever;
The mountains stretched their necks o'erhead,
    To see their image in the river!

THE WORKINGMAN'S WIFE.

FROM day to day, from morn till night,
   She works with an earnest will,
To make the home look clean and bright—
   Her mission on earth fulfil.

No selfish thought pervades her mind,
   In "HOME" is her great delight;
By look, and word, and tone so kind,
   She leads her children aright.

The best the cupboard can afford
   For her husband she prepares,
Well content with a kindly word,
   As reward for all her cares.

The children know a tender spot
   For them in her heart is given;—
Her Lord hath said—" Forbid them not,
   Of such the kingdom of Heaven."

The day will come when mother's face
   Shall be white and cold as snow;
No one on earth can fill her place,
   Her value we then shall know.

Hark! how she pleads in earnest pray'r
   That God would her dear ones save;
Oh, seek then to lighten her care—
   Brighten her path to the grave!

DINNA HIDE THE HEART-LOVE!

Oh! dinna hide the heart-love,
   Speak it oot!—tell it oot!
A' guid thochts come frae above,
   O' that there is nae doot!

Whan the heart wi' love is fu',
   Rinnin' ower!—rinnin' ower!
Let some draps like Heaven's dew,
   Wat some wee thirsty flower!

Licht the sunshine o' yer face,
   Wi' a smile!—wi' a smile!
Gie nae sorrow there a place
   Life's happiness to spoil!

Angry words cut like a sword,
   Brither, mine!—sister, mine!
Speak the honest, kindly word,
   To mak' leal hearts entwine!

Life at best is unco short,
   Mak' it guid!—mak' it guid!
Hurtin' feelin's is nae sport,
   Aft causin' hearts to bluid!

Lift the fallen, shield the weak,
   A' ye can!—a' ye can!
Aye some word o' comfort speak,
   To cheer your brither—man!

Miscellaneous Poems.

Miscellaneous.

A SUMMER'S DAY;
OR,
MORNING, NOON, AND NIGHT.

Introduction.

SPRING show'rs have wash'd the winter snows away,
And Nature smiles at the approach of May,
Clad in the brightest green, and deck'd with flowers,
Which speak of balmy winds and sunny hours;
When birds, and bees, and butterflies abound,
And flowers in rich profusion deck the ground,
Strewn here and there by Flora's wanton hand,
And Hope sings merrily o'er all the land;
  Oh! then, 'tis surely summer!

I.—MORNING.

TIS morning! for the rising sun
  His daily journey hath begun;
Flooding the earth with glory bright,
Chasing away the gloom of night;

Closing the eye of every star
That twinkles in the heavens afar;
Paling the moon's soft, silvery light,
Till it recedes from mortal sight!

All hail! thou ruler of the day,
Nature delights to own thy sway;
At thy approach the smallest flower
On hill, or dale, or verdant bower,
Lifts up its head, though wet with dew,
And spreads its petals out to view,
To cheer the heart, and glad the eyes,
A dainty morning sacrifice!

At Sol's glad light the feather'd throng
Make woods resound with cheerful song,
And, full of grateful, glad surprise,
Fly out to meet thee in the skies;
The milkmaid sings a merry lay,
As through the fields of fragrant hay
She gaily trips to meet the cows,
Whose welcome noise the echoes rouse.

Sweet morning hours!—first-fruit of day—
None but the slothful spurn away
Thy gifts of beauty, health, and light,
And, slumb'ring, turn thee into night!
When glory gilds the eastern sky,
And Nature lifts her voice on high,
Why should not man, with grateful heart,
Join in and take a noble part?

II.—NOON.

THE sun hath reached meridian's height,
And robed the earth in glory bright;
Flora, arrayed in all her charms,
Looks up and smiles; with loving arms
Seeks to invite his presence near,
Like perfect love which hath no fear,
And thinks no evil, though now a show'r
Should hide his face in noontide's hour!

Bright noon! when all around is life,
And hum, and stir, and busy strife;
Nature, in all her various forms—
Like angry waves in wintry storms—
Strives life with life for daily bread,
For all must live and all be fed,
Each eager to secure a prey
Before noontide shall pass away!

The butterfly enjoys the hour,
And sips sweet nectar from the flower;
The humble bee doth homeward bring
Her treasures sweet on laden wing;
The cheerful sparrow on the ground
A dainty mid-day meal hath found,—
All nature knows the time of day,
Nor lets it idly pass away!

'Tis noon! and from the village school
A joyous host, released from rule,
Rush out with hearts as light as air,
Without a sorrow or a care,
But to improve the fleeting hour
Whether in sunshine or in shower,
For noon's short hour flies fast away
When given to joyous mirth and play!

III.—NIGHT.

THE evening shades are falling fast,
Long shadows on the ground are cast,
The western sky is all aglow
With fiery glory setting low;
The hill-tops glance with changing hue,
A noble back-ground to the view,
As mountain, river, lake, and plain,
Are bathed in glory once again!

Sweet evening hours! suggesting rest,
To weary toilers thou art blest;
See yonder cottage at whose door
The children look for "Pa" once more,
And by the welcome they impart
Bid all the cares of day depart;
Domestic joys are life's sweet flowers,
Full blooming in the evening hours;

MISCELLANEOUS.

As evening deepens into night,
A host of stars shed purest light;
Fair Luna comes upon the scene,
With halo of bright, silv'ry sheen,
To woo the lover out to stroll
The shady walks with love-lit soul,
And pour into the maiden ear
The soulful words she loves to hear!

At last the midnight hour is past,
The stillness of the grave is cast
On all around with potent spell,—
The day is past and all is well!
For Israel's God doth ever keep
His watchful eye o'er those who sleep;
Tired Nature rests, while God alone
With heavenly love protects His own!

LIFE'S SUPREME MOMENTS.

I.

WHEN first to earth a living soul is brought,
  Out of the depths of darkness, doubt, and
    pain,
Ere yet its being hath the power of thought
  To measure life as either loss or gain ;
Our time of birth is moment most supreme,
  Call'd into being by the will of God,
To wond'ring angels a delightful theme,
  From first to last to mark the pathway trod !

II.

Another moment most supreme is when
  The lisping infant stammers out "Mamma !"
Or, when the father, coming home at e'en,
  Hears baby-lips lisp out the first " Papa ! "
Oh, these are moments when the heart beats fast
  With ecstasy and fond parental love,
The sweets of life are all too short to last,
  Else would we never sigh for those above !

III.

When first the human mind grasps holy things,
  And God is known and felt within the soul,
'Tis then the blood-bought one exults and sings
  The praise of Him who doth our lives control ;
That is a moment of supremest joy
  Which feels the transfer of our heart to God ;
To bless and praise Him is its lov'd employ,
  Even to the kissing of His chast'ning rod !

IV.

Whene'er our heart is sore with bitter grief,
   And clouds of darkness seem to hover near,
'Tis then we find in prayer a sweet relief,
   An antidote to each dark doubt and fear;
These are sweet moments that we call supreme
   When soul and body seem to soar on high,
And bask contented in some heavenly theme,
   When God, and Love, and Purity are nigh!

V.

The memory of school-days!—how they tint
   Our after-years with sunshine and delight;
School is to life the intellectual mint
   From whence is won the stamp of genius bright;
Where, after many sessions wisely spent,
   Comes forth the youth to battle with his fate:
Those knowing most with knowledge less content
   Than those whose lesser knowledge makes elate!

VI.

It is a moment most supreme to find
   That Wisdom is the currency of heaven,
And that to cultivate the human mind
   To those who would be wise the taste is given;
Knowledge is true greatness—the mind expands
   And oft is index'd on the human face;
He is most humble who most understands
   And nearest God who loves His law to trace!

VII.

Oh, Love! thou art the elixir of life,
　The sweet'ning draught in sorrow's bitter cup,
An antidote to selfishness and strife—
　Humbling the proud, the humble raising up!
When love at first beholds its counterpart
　The die is cast for future peace or pain,
'Tis answered by a fluttering of the heart—
　This " supreme moment " never comes again!

VIII.

Oh, happy state! the only life complete,
　Two loving hearts in one pure purpose bent,
God's wise provision for communion sweet,—
　Felicity and love, with sweet content;
Love is the keynote of a happy life,
　To which fond hearts in unison accord,
Heaven's greatest gift to man—a loving wife,
　" Tender and true " in every thought and word!

IX.

Thus portion'd out, life is a pleasant dream,
　Though here and there some trials intervene;
No clouds without some bright and hopeful gleam,
　With rays of sunshine darting in between!
In every life supreme sweet moments come,
　Like sunshine after rain enjoy'd the more,—
A deed, a word, a look, a smile to some
　May echoes wake to live for evermore!

X.

As there are moments of supremest joy,
  So there are seasons of deep inward pain—
Sometimes ingratitude our hearts annoy,
  Sometimes we lose when all our plans were gain!
Such is the sum of human smiles and tears,
  But we might often smile, instead of weep;
And such the record of our hopes and fears,
  Instead of anxious vigils—we might sleep!

XI.

If that our life were hid with Christ in God,
  We might defy the rocks and shoals of life!
If we would walk the path that Jesus trod,
  We might be spared much anxious care and strife;
So, that, at last, our closing moments near,
  They might be those of supreme happiness,
Despoil'd of every doubt, care, grief, or fear,
  Such is the entrance to the gates of bliss!

XII.

Death is a blessing when it comes with peace,
  And frees the soul from all its suff'ring clay;
To die is gain when Death but brings release,
  And turns our darkness into endless day!
Oh! moment most supreme when first a soul
  Beholds its Saviour face to face in Heaven,
And finds its name inscribed upon the scroll
  Reserved for those who for "the prize" have striven!

NATURE'S TEMPLE.

'TIS sweet to sit in pensive mood,
'Mid Nature's grand, stern solitude,
Where warbling birds pour forth their lays,
In happy, joyous songs of praise.

Or watch some noble cat'ract bound
From giddy height to lowly ground,
Where echoes ring from peak to peak,
And God in Nature seems to speak.

With praise to God the woods resound,
Surrounding hills repeat the sound,
And in my heart an echo rings,
Which joy and consolation brings.

There doth my soul find sweet relief,
And gather strength for future grief;
For life's stern duties now prepare,
By supplicating God in prayer.

Oh, God! to be alone with Thee,
In Nature's Temple—rich and free;
And for a time forget the strife
Of man with man—of Death with Life.

Oh, happy hour! oh, sweet retreat!
With Thee, my Father, thus to meet;
And learn from Nature to adore
The God of Nature evermore!

NATURE'S TEMPLE.

Or watch some noble cataract bound
From giddy height to lowly ground,
Where echoes ring from peak to peak,
And God in Nature seems to speak.

A CHRISTMAS CAROL.

1. Ring out the merry Christmas bell That tells of joy and gladness, Our happy hearts with pleasure swell, This is no time for sadness; This is the crowning of the year, A day of merry-making, With feast and song our hearts we'll cheer, All anxious cares forsaking.

A CHRISTMAS CAROL.

RING out the merry Christmas bell
  That tells of joy and gladness.
Our happy hearts with pleasure swell,
  This is no time for sadness;
This is the crowning of the year,
  A day of merry-making,
With feast and song our hearts we'll cheer,
  All anxious cares forsaking.

'Twas Christmas-tide when Jesus lay
  All lowly in a manger,
He came to take our sins away,
  And save our souls from danger;
The shepherds on the hills at dawn
  Heard angel-voices singing:
"Now peace on earth, goodwill to men,
  We are this morning bringing."

'Tis eighteen hundred years and more
  Since that glad Christmas morning,
Yet once a year, on every shore,
  Are happy hearts adorning
The Christmas tree with presents rare,
  Its dark-green boughs are laden,
And round it dance the children fair,
  The lover and the maiden!

Oh! merry, happy Christmas Day,
　For young and old together,
The very snow-flakes seem more gay,
　Though bitter cold the weather;
As round the family fireside
　The dear ones we are meeting,
Let peace and harmony abide,
　With love each other greeting.

MISCELLANEOUS.

FAITH ILLUSTRATED.

THE night was calm and still, the moon shone
    bright,
And lent the silver-sweetness of her light
To guide the lonely patrol on his beat,
As, with a measured step, from street to street,
His echoing footsteps beat a solemn tread;
And from the city towers, far over head,
The midnight hour rang out with mournful chime,
Telling the wakeful of the march of time.

But hark! what awful sound is that I hear,
Which falls like thunder on my closing ear?—
Fire! *fire!* FIRE! 'tis the patrol's warning cry
That rings from house to house, from earth to sky,
Rousing the wakeful, scattering the dreams
Of love and joy, and for a moment gleams
From face to face—from eye to eye—
A terror as of death or danger nigh.

Fire! *fire!* FIRE! onward press the anxious crowd,
With rushing, hasty steps, and noises loud,
To yonder mansion, where the ruddy glare
Speaks louder than the groans of dark despair!
The greedy flames surround with furious power
The doomed abode; and in that midnight hour
Strong men are weak, and none but they are brave
Who look to Him whose power alone can save.

Thus felt a father when he saw his child,
Far out of human reach, 'mid danger wild,
On top-most storey, and in blank despair,
His piteous cries resounding through the air.
At last he heard his father's well-known voice,
Which made his sinking heart with hope rejoice,—
"Spring to my arms, my son! do not delay,
Haste! haste! and I shall bear thee safe away!"

The brave child heard and, stepping on the sill,
Prepared to execute his father's will;
He looked from death to life with anxious eyes,
And ceased his murmur and despairing cries.
Then, with his tiny arms outstretched to Heaven,
Heroic courage to his soul was given;
He, fearless, sprang from all the dread alarms,
And fainting, dropped into his father's arms.

O let such FAITH be mine,—such childlike faith
In Thee, O God; then neither fear nor scathe
Shall hinder me from clinging to Thine arm,
For Thou alone canst save from fear or harm!
And when, at last, *Thy call* from earth I hear,
No doubt shall hinder, nor despairing fear;
But, looking up to Thee with heart and eyes,
Thou wilt accept and bear me to the skies!

MISCELLANEOUS.

A BIRTHDAY GREETING.

TIME is ever on the wing,
　　Fast our moments fly away;
Let us prize them, though they bring
　　Joy and sorrow mixed alway!
Had we joy alone, my friend,
　　We would seek no other sphere;
Did God only sorrow send,
　　We would wish the end was near!

God is wiser far than we,
　　And He knoweth what is best;
Let us in His wisdom see
　　That He seeks our FAITH to test!
May we live, as though this hour
　　Were our last on earth to spend;
And, come sunshine, shade, or show'r,
　　God's best blessing will attend!

Let the years roll on apace,
　　Heaven is nearer than before;
Let us bravely trials face,
　　Waves break loudest near the shore!
Summer, Autumn, Winter, Spring,
　　All within one year are bound;
Let us through each season sing
　　Songs of praise the whole year round!

FLOWERS!

FLOWERS are loved by young and old,
As they gracefully unfold
Sweetness caught from Eden's bowers,
When at first God made the flowers:
Rich in every tint and hue,
Smiling through their tears of dew;
Beauty's glory crowns their head,
As they peep from grassy bed!

Purity the Lily seems,
As she in the sunlight gleams;
Humility the Pansy knows,
Happiness bespeaks the Rose,
Love the laughing Daffodil,
Pinks our eyes with *Beauty* fill;
Every flower, a charm its own,
Fills a place on Flora's throne!

Flowers may teach the heart of man,
As no other teacher can:
God's creative hand was there,
When He made the flowers so fair;

MISCELLANEOUS.

Out of chaos formed the earth,
Spake, and planets had their birth;
To adorn the human race,
Lent the beauty of His face!

He who loves the tiny flower
Something knows of Heaven's power,
Which will hope and courage give,
Strength and sweetness while he live;
Like the flowers we pass away,
Short, yet sweet, is life's brief day—
Let good deeds and thoughts sublime,
Stand the touch and test of time!

SONG OF THE " DRUMMER."

SING you the song of the " drummer " bold,
  Who sighs for the comforts of home ;
But goods must be bought, and goods must be sold,
  And therefore the " drummer " must roam !

CHORUS—
  All aboard going East ! all aboard going West !
    Is the cry that I often hear ;
  And my hobby, I confess, is to travel by express,
    And of accidents I have no fear !

I'm happy and gay to " spot a live town,"
  Where business is "booming," you know !
While humming a song my " samples " lay down,
  And manage to make "a good show ! "— CHORUS.

When customers come I welcome them all
  To " sample rooms " in my hotel ;
I'm proud to see them, and they like to call,
  I treat all my patrons so well !—CHORUS.

I live " by the way," yet fare very well,
  Some flirting I do if I can !
Of these escapades I'm not going to tell,
  For that is not down in my plan.—CHORUS.

In commerce and trade it is hard to compete,
  Quotations are " 'way down below ;"
When I " take the road," I'm not to be beat,
  Good orders I always can show !—CHORUS.

MISCELLANEOUS.

SONG OF THE "DRUMMER."

Copyright. Music by Prof. J. F. Johnstone, Toronto.

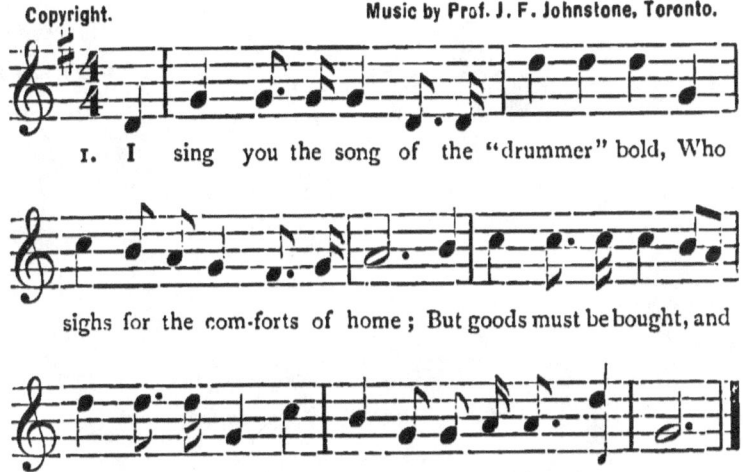

1. I sing you the song of the "drummer" bold, Who sighs for the com-forts of home; But goods must be bought, and goods must be sold, And therefore the "drummer" must roam!

CHORUS.

"All a-board going East! all a-board going West!" Is the

cry that I of-ten hear; And my hob-by, I con-fess, is to

tra-vel by express, And of ac-ci-dents I have no fear!

LIFE'S PROGRESS.

Rivers rolling to the sea
　Loose themselves in ocean,
Bearing on their bosoms free
　Noble ships in motion.
　* 　* 　* 　* 　* 　* 　*

Ah! soon we'll reach life's ocean strand,
　Just like the winding river,
Safe in the hollow of that Hand
　Which holds the seas for ever.

MISCELLANEOUS.

LIFE'S PROGRESS.

DOWN the mountains, down the hills,
  Trickling on for ever;
Gentle springs make little rills,
  Little rills the river.

Rivers rolling to the sea
  Lose themselves in ocean,
Bearing on their bosoms free
  Noble ships in motion.

Such is life, a constant change,
  Still from small to greater;
Let us learn the lesson strange
  Taught by our Creator:

Life is giv'n for noble ends,
  Lofty thoughts and actions,
Winning to our bosom—friends
  Gain'd in life's transactions.

Ah! soon we'll reach life's ocean strand,
  Just like the mighty river,
Safe in the hollow of that Hand
  Which holds the seas for ever.

TO THE PANSY.

OH, Pansy! with the velvet hue,
And spots of gold, and pearly dew;
How gracefully you hang your head,
Scarce rais'd above your humble bed.

I love you for your queenly grace,
Your happy smile, your winsome face;
In sweet retreats you love to dwell,
And lend the vale thy beauty-spell.

Sweet emblem of a "heart at ease,"*
Thy form my inmost fancies please;
In quiet beauty you excel
All other flowers in wood or dell.

Thou mightest well be Flora's queen,
If thou wouldst let thy charms be seen;
And seek to vie with other flowers
That deck with beauty kingly bowers.

But thou art wise to grace the spot
Where God has cast thy humble lot;
And there, secure from rude alarms,
Display thy modest, winsome charms!

When I look up from thee to God,
And see His glory in the sod,
My heart in sweet tranquility
Would learn from thee "HUMILITY!"

---

* This flower is sometimes called "Heart's-ease."

A LESSON FROM THE CLOCK.

TICK, tick, tick, tick,
Time flies so quick,
With never ceaseless motion;
   Our moments pass
   Like sands in glass,
Or wavelets of the ocean.

   Thus moments go,
   For weal or woe,
And none returneth ever;
   How mindful we
   Should ever be
To spend with wise endeavour.

   The life of man
   Is but a span,
Short, transient, and fleeting;
   With here and there
   A joy or care,
A parting or a meeting.

   Then let each hour,
   Like beauteous flower,
Some fragrance send to Heaven;
   To God above,
   In grateful love,
Let ransomed powers be given.

MYSTERY!

BIRTH of a soul! what mystery
   Enwraps thy silent history,—
     In dumb amaze
     We stand and gaze,
Own baffled with thy mystery!

Oh, Love! thou art a mystery,
   Yet old as earth's dim history,—
     From birth till death
     We feel thy breath,
Oh, wistful, blissful mystery!

Oh, Life, thou art a mystery!
   Each living soul a history
     Of hopes and fears,
     Of joys and tears,—
An ever-present mystery!

Oh, heart of man! thy history
   Is oft enshrin'd in mystery,—
     Yet God can scan
     The heart of man
And flood with light its mystery.

Oh, death! thou art a mystery,
Who knows thy after-history?
    From heaven or hell
    None come to tell
The living of thy mystery.

Oh, Life beyond! Oh, mystery!
We yet shall know thy history,—
    So live each day,
    That, come what may,
Our souls shall fear no mystery.

Oh, realms of bliss! what mystery
Enshrouds thy sphere and history,—
    No finite eyes
    Can pierce the skies
To scan thy blissful mystery.

Oh, God! Thou art a mystery,
Thy love a world's history,—
    Most humbly we
    Shall worship Thee,
Till Thou shalt solve all mystery!

TWO POOR ORPHAN BOYS.

GOD help poor orphans, for they need
Our Father's watchful care indeed;
Out in the cold wide world alone,
Where strangers speak with freezing tone;
With none to take them to their heart,
Or dry the burning tears that start
From sunken eyes and hollow cheek,
Which want, neglect, and hunger speak.

Two years ago their father died,
And soon their mother, by his side
In one cold grave was laid at rest,
And join'd the everlasting blest;
The greatest pain she felt at death
Was whisper'd with her dying breath:
" God keep my boys when I am gone,
Poor, helpless orphans, all alone !"

Ah ! how they struggl'd for their bread,
And oft went supperless to bed ;
And, sometimes, neither bed nor board
Their scanty pittance could afford.
Oft in the storm, and snow, and sleet,
They travell'd on with cold, wet feet,
And sought that kindly passers-by
Would pity the poor orphans' cry !

Sometimes a crossing neatly swept,
By one at either end, was kept.
Where, now and then, an honest cent
Was earned by them with great content.
As long as work is brisk they feel
No evil tempting them to steal,
Or beg, or whine, or seem dismay'd,
Or of their lot feel half afraid.

Dear Christian people, help such boys,
Who little know of earthly joys:
Do speak to them with kindly tone,
And make the orphan's cause your own;
Try if your purse can spare a cent—
Or e'en a dime—to God 'tis lent,
And make their sad and painful lot
By kindness almost half forgot!

LAUGHING.

OH, how I love the hearty laugh
    That rings with a merry peal!
The outcome of some witty "chaff,"
    Which makes one cheerful feel;
A laugh which almost racks the jaw,
    A regular side-splitter!
In which all join with "loud guffaw,"
    And nothing in't that's bitter!

I love when children laugh outright,
    And shout in their playful glee,
When all run out to see the sight,
    Or join in the sport so free!
A laugh that knows not care or ill,
    The frolicsome laugh of fun!
Which speaks of naught but right good-will,
    As they skip, and laugh, and run!

I hate the haughty laugh of scorn,
    From the dudish fops called "*men*,"
Who sneer at worth if humbly born,
    And smile at "the upper ten!"
Whose empty laugh shows lack of brain
    Their language devoid of wit,
Their greatest feat to "twirl a cane,"
    Or display "*a perfect fit!*"

AN HONEST MAN.

"An honest man's the noblest work of God."—*Burns.*

SHEW me the man of true and honest heart,
Who, for the sake of gain, will not depart
From paths of rectitude, and then I can
Shew you God's noblest work—
An honest man!

Temptation's darts do not disturb his mind,
True to himself he's true to all mankind,
By honest toil he earns whate'er he can,
And proves himself to be—
An honest man!

Truth is his watchword—lips that speak no guile,
His face illumin'd with an honest smile,
Looks eye to eye with ours, nor fails to scan
The traits and signs which mark—
The honest man!

God bless the honest man whose bosom thrills
With love and sympathy for others' ills,
And "robs" himself of ease if so he can,
With woman's tenderness, display—
"The man!"

The world is full of sin, and vice, and crime,
But honesty will stand the test of time;
Truth, Virtue, Charity, shall lead the van,—
God's name is honour'd by—
The honest man!

THE POWER OF SONG.

THE poet's heart is ever young,
  His thoughts are light and gay;
To Nature's praise his harp is strung
  In sweetest harmony.

The minstrel's soul is all aflame
  With passion's holy fire;
He courts the Muse in love's sweet name,
  And kindles with desire.

He joins the children in their play,
  And pleases them with song;
He soothes them off to sleep alway,
  With lullabies of song.

His heart is touch'd with others' woe
  In deepest sympathy:
His tears with theirs together flow
  In tuneful symphony.

For tyrant-threats he hath no fear,
  But wages bitter strife
With all that dares to interfere
  With liberty and life.

The soldier on the tented fiel
  Feels that his cause is strong,
For Freedom's enemy must yield
  Before the Patriot's song.

The sailor on the stormy sea
  Beguiles the hour with song,
As, whistling for the winds so free,
  He steers his bark along.

The reapers by the waving corn
  Doth make the welkin ring,
And when the harvest home is borne
  The harvest-song they sing.

The power of song to stir the soul,
  Or soothe the human heart,
Is felt by man from pole to pole,
  Or distant isles apart.

Like notes from Heaven's angelic choir,
  Or herald-angel's song,
Our minstrels, with poetic fire,
  The echoes still prolong!

THE LITTLE NEWSPAPER BOYS.

TWO little brothers left their home
   One cold, bleak winter's day,
All round the city streets to roam,
   But not in childish play.

They on a noble errand went,
   An honest dime to gain,
By selling papers—well content
   To brave the sleet and rain.

One ten year's old was brother "Bill,"
   And six year's old was "Jack;"
They trudged along with right good-will,
   Though business was quite slack!

Yet bravely shouts the elder boy:
   "My papers! who will buy?"
And at each sale a smile of joy
   Lights up each cheerful eye.

The weary hours of night wore past,
   The steeple clock struck Nine:
One bun between them eased their fast,
   But Jack began to pine.

"Oh! Bill, I'm tired and sleepy now,
   I'll sit down here and rest;"
And soon the cold and chilly brow
   Dropp'd feebly on his breast.

MISCELLANEOUS.

His brother Bill, with courage high,
    More energy display'd,
"The latest news!" did loudly cry,
    Not daunted or afraid.

Yet, now and then, dear little Jack
    Would look with tearful eye
On brother Bill, as he came back
    To tell him—"not to cry!"

"I've nearly sold them all now, Jack,
    There's only three to sell;
When they are sold, high on my back
    I'll ride you home pell-mell!"

At last their merchandise was gone,
    Ten cents was fairly won!
And Bill knelt down to help Jack on
    His back, for the home-run!

Dear Christian people, help such boys
    To earn an honest cent,
They little know of earthly joys,
    And yet seem well content!

ROSEDALE.

TORONTO'S SYLVAN SUBURB.

BONNIE Rosedale ! I must sing
   Of thy beauty rare,
By the stream meandering
   Through thy valleys fair ;
Thou are truly nature's book
   Bound in living green,
Hill and dale and quiet nook—
   Home of Flora's queen.

Here the swallows first appear
   Telling us of spring,
Early snow-drops seek to cheer—
   Birds to build and sing !
Here the young leaves first embower
   Thy fairy-like ravine,
First to bud and last to flower
   Nature here is seen.

Sweet to walk thy leafy glade
  'Neath the silver moon,
There the lover and the maid
  Find their hearts in tune
To the music and the words
  Of a lover's dream,
To the singing of the birds
  And the whispering stream.

Bonnie Rosedale ! sweet retreat
  From the city's din,
From its toil, and dust, and heat,
  Let me enter in ;
There to revel in thy beauty,
  Wreaths of praise entwine,
Gather strength for toil and duty,
  At thy sylvan shrine !

TO THE FOUR WINDS OF HEAVEN.

OH ! cold NORTH WIND from the Polar seas,
  Thy breath congeals lake, brook, and river ;
You strip the leaves from the tallest trees,
  And make them bend, and sigh, and quiver !

Oh ! blow, SOUTH WIND from the coral strand,
  Thy breath is sweet with the flowers' perfume ;
Thrice welcome thou to our cold North land,
  To cheer our hearts with the rose's bloom !

Oh ! blow, EAST WIND, with thy favouring gales,
  To speed our ships from the mother-lands ;
And glad our eyes with the full-blown sails,
  That bring to our shores brave hearts and hands !

Oh ! blow, WEST WIND, with thy fresh, strong breeze,
  Prepare our frames for the frost and snow ;
Shake down the ripe fruits from off the trees,
  And tinge our cheeks with health's ruddy glow !

God tempers the winds for life or death,
  As over the earth they sweeping go ;
He speaks in the zephyr's balmy breath,
  As well as when loudest tempests blow.

THE KNIGHTS OF LABOUR.

A power has risen in the land,
Who work together hand-in-hand,
A noble, energetic band,—
    The Knights of Labour.

Monopoly must not control
The labour market, heart and soul,
And seek to pay with meagre dole
    The Knights of Labour.

Let man to man this maxim tell:
" He doeth right who worketh well,
And ought to best advantage sell
    His wealth of labour!"

Though wealth be strong, yet right is might,
And victory shall crown the right,—
All honour to your noble fight,
    Brave Knights of Labour!

While enterprise we will respect,
Our rights we never shall neglect;
All tyranny we must reject
    While Knights of Labour!

LIFE'S BRIGHTER SIDE.

'TIS better to smile than to frown,
   'Tis better to laugh than to cry;
Then, don't let your spirits get down,
   And never say "fail" tho' you die!

Though trouble like mountains arise,
   And fortune seems hard to attain,
Look hopefully up to the skies,
   For sunshine will come after rain.

Those taught in adversity's school
   Are braver and better by far;
The cowardly man, as a rule,
   Is not to be trusted in war.

A brave heart is sure to succeed,
   The weak one will go to the wall;
And God will assist those indeed
   Who help themselves up when they fall.

If in love affections are bent,
   And wooing is met with disdain,
Bear up with apparent content,
   And time will restore you again!

The world is more full of joy
   Than most people care to admit;
If usefully time you'll employ,
   Life's trials won't hurt you a bit!

SOAP-BUBBLES.

WHAT a happy holiday,
Brothers Jack and Will at play;
Blowing bubbles light as air,
Chasing them o'er stool and chair!
As they blow, each ruddy cheek
Happiness and joy bespeak;
Each the other tries to "chaff"—
Hard to blow when forc'd to laugh!

Little "pussy" likes the fun,
Swift across the floor to run,
When they break across her eyes,
Gets "her back up" in surprise!
Tasting soap in mouth and nose,
Sniffing to a corner goes;
Till another tempts her out,
Once again to run about!

Mamma hears the noisy din,
Slyly at the door peeps in;
But she loves to see them play,
Happy in their joy alway!
Swift a thought across her mind
Utterance finds in words so kind:—
Ah! my boys, a moral see
From the bubbles light and free:

Empty bubbles, light as air,
For a moment bright and fair;
Some ascend like stars to heaven,
Some to swift destruction driven;
If thou would'st escape each snare,
Guard thy life with constant prayer;
God will waft thee to the skies,
Float thee into Paradise!

HAPPY CHILDHOOD.

HAPPY childhood, full of smiles,
    All the livelong day;
Winsome ways and cunning wiles,
    Ever fond of play.

How our hearts with pleasure beat,
    Feeling young and gay;
When we see them on the street,
    Sadness flies away!

Care or sorrow hath no part
    In life's early day,
Thine the light and happy heart,
    Singing merrily!

Like the flowers of early Spring
    O'er the meadows cast,
Sweetness to our hearts they bring,
    Dear mem'ries of the past.

But the future, who can tell
    What their lot may be?
God, who doeth all things well,
    Keep them pure and free!

MISCELLANEOUS.

KNIGHTS OF PYTHIAS.

COME, Knights of Pythias, all combine,
Let Friendship, Truth, and Love entwine;
Our noble deeds, with one accord,
Shall conquests make that shame the sword!
CHORUS.—Come, join together heart and hand,
  United we shall ever stand;
  Encircle earth by sea and land,
  With Friendship's loving golden band!

Our Order stands the test of time,—
A foe to falsehood, want, and crime;
A band of brothers, brave and free,
The "Golden Rule" our only plea!
   CHORUS.—"Come join," etc.

The widows' and the orphans' cause
Are part and parcel of our laws;
We help the needy, shield the weak,
And words of sympathy we speak.
   CHORUS.—"Come join," etc.

Should dire Oppression's iron hand
Be laid upon our native land,
Our swords shall strike the tyrant low,
And Freedom smile at every blow!
   CHORUS.—"Come join," etc.

MISCELLANEOUS.

KNIGHTS OF PYTHIAS.

Maestoso. Music by Prof. J. F. Johnstone, Toronto.

1. Come, Knights of Pyth-ias, all com-bine, Let Friendship, Truth, and Love entwine; Our no-ble deeds, with one ac-cord, Shall con-quests make that shame the sword!

CHORUS.

Come, join to-geth-er heart and hand, U-ni-ted we shall ev-er stand; En-cir-cle earth by sea and land, With Friendship's lov-ing gold-en band.

THE YOUNG MUSICIAN.

Copyrighted.
Simply.

Music by Prof. J. F. Johnstone,
Toronto.

A, B, C, D, E, F, G, That's the scale as you may see;

On the lines and in the space; Each in or-der you may trace!

CHORUS.

A, B, C, D, E, F, G, A mu-sic-ian I would be;

Oh, it is such mer-ry fun, Up and down the scale to run!

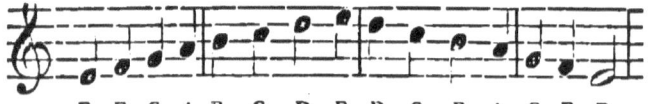

E, F, G, A, B, C, D, E, D, C, B, A, G, F, E,

Oh, it is such mer-ry fun, Up and down the scale to run!

THE YOUNG MUSICIAN.

A,—B,—C,—D,—E,—F,—G,
That's "*the scale*," as you may see;
On the "*lines*" and in the "*space*,"
Each in order you may trace!

CHORUS.—A,—B,—C,—D,—E,—F,—G,
  A musician I would be;
  Oh, it is such merry fun
  Up and down "the scale" to run!

E,—G,—B,—D,—F,—on "*lines*,"
Learn by sight the useful signs;
F,—A,—C,—E,—in the "*space*,"
Don't forget the spelling—FACE!

CHORUS.—"A, B, C, D, E, F, G," etc.

Notes are simply "*signs*" you see,
Round and black as black can be;
From the perfect number "*seven*,"
Each its proper place is given!

CHORUS.—"A, B, C, D, E, F, G," etc.

"*Sharps*" and "*flats*" some patience need,
If at music you'd succeed;
But "*sweet melody*" is there,
When you take great pains and care!
CHORUS.—"A, B, C, D, E, F, G," etc.

Soon my little friend may try
Something greater by-and-by,
If her teacher she obeys,
And remembers all he says!
CHORUS.—"A, B, C, D, E, F, G," etc.

Just be patient—never fret,
Or into a passion get;
Else "*a discord*" you will make,
Which would be "*a great mistake!*"
CHORUS.—"A, B, C, D, E, F, G," etc.

THE YOUNG MUSICIAN.

Just be patient—never fret,
Or into a passion get:
Else "*a discord*" you will make,
Which would be "*a great mistake!*"

CHORUS.—A,—B,—C,—D,—E,—F,—G,
 A musician I would be;
 Oh, it is such merry fun
 Up and down "the scale" to run!

SHE PAYS HER DEBTS WITH KISSES!

I KNOW a winsome little pet
    With wealth of roseate blisses,
Who takes what favors she can get,
    And pays her debts with—kisses!

At night when I come home to tea
    She bribes me with her "kishes,"
Then plants herself upon my knee
    And tastes of all my dishes!

She comes off best in every "trade,"
    And seldom ever misses
To catch me in the trap she's laid,
    Then "pays me off" with—kisses!

She says she wants a "dolly" nice,
    With long and golden tresses,
And if I ask her for the price,
    Gives kisses and caresses!

I dearly love this little maid,
    Above all other misses;
I'll take back every word I've said
    And "trade" with her for—"TISSES!"

SHE PAYS HER DEBTS WITH KISSES.

At night when I come home to tea
She bribes me with her "kishes,"
Then plants herself upon my knee
And tastes of all my dishes!

THE WORKINGMAN'S HALF-HOLIDAY.

GOD bless the men of means who try
   To sweeten Labour's cup,
By list'ning to the earnest cry
   To lift "the masses up"
Above the drudgery of life,
   The needful hours to spare,
A short respite from busy strife,
   Sweet Nature's joys to share!

'Twill prove the best investment sure,
   These hours to toilers given,
'Twill tend to make them good and pure,
   And pave their way to Heaven;
Respect and honesty will spring
   From hearts made glad and free,
To duty more attention bring,
   Thy grateful servants be.

And, then, what pleasure to thy heart,
   To mark the happy faces,
As pleasure parties gaily start
   For rural, healthy places,
To breathe the sweet pure air of heaven,
   By mountain, lake or river,
And use the means thus kindly given
   As best would please the giver!

MISCELLANEOUS.

Then give without a grudge or fear
  The boon so much desired,
The patient wife and children dear
  With hope shall feel inspired;
Life shall be then worth living for,
  Dull care shall fly away,
And once a week no cloud shall mar
  Their glad half-holiday!

THE DYING CHILD.

BESIDE the death-bed of her child
  A mother bent in grief,
But to her pain and anguish wild
  There came a sweet relief.

The dying child, in accents mild,
  And full of tender love,
The silence broke while thus she spoke
  Of brighter scenes above:

"Oh, mother dear, you need not fear
  Nor fret yourself for me,
Dry from your cheek the falling tear,
  I soon shall happy be.

"I soon shall reach that 'happy land,'
  And join that blessed throng,
Who ever stand at God's right hand
  Singing the angels' song.

"I'll wait for you and father dear
  On that bright, happy shore,
Where death nor sorrow cometh near,
  And friends depart no more.

"Then let me go—I must not stay,
  I hear my Saviour's voice;
The angels beckon me away,
  And bid my soul rejoice."

The angels fair have come and gone,
  They bore that child away;
Another soul is at the throne,
  Here but the lifeless clay.

Oh, friends bereaved, weep not for those
  Whom Jesus died to save;
Through Him they conquer'd all their foes
  And triumphed o'er the grave!

ON MY FORTIETH BIRTHDAY.

FORTY years of age to-day!
Ah! how time doth pass away;
Like a pleasant summer's day,
Or like children's hours of play!

Now I've reach'd ripe manhood's prime,
Fain would bar the march of time;
Raven locks now tipp'd with grey,
Show the signs of sure decay.

Grateful love my heart doth fill,—
Reach'd the summit of life's hill;
Safe through many an anxious care,
"*Thank Thee, Lord,*" my daily prayer.

Now a-down "life's other side,"
Knowing not what may betide;
Trusting where I cannot trace,
Till I see God face to face!

Let the years, then, come and go,
Fraught with weal or mix'd with woe;
I will trust my Father's love
Till I reach His home above!

PRIDE.

PRIDE is Satan's favourite plant,
    A noxious weed infernal;
A passion-flower of waste and want,
    To poison souls eternal!

How foolish is the pride of man,
    The creature of a day,
Whose life is measur'd by a span,
    And then returns to clay!

When first our eyes beheld the light
    No claim to pomp had we;
All men are equal in God's sight,
    Sustain'd, belov'd, and free!

Our Saviour died for all mankind,
    A full and free salvation;
Then why should we be so unkind,
    As sneer at dress or station?

The Son of God had humble birth,
    Yet now He reigns in Heaven;
Those who oppress the poor on earth
    Shall from His throne be driven!

LOVE AND SYMPATHY.

THE balm of sympathy how sweet
   In trial's pensive hour,
When wave on wave of sorrows beat,
   And clouds of darkness lower.

'Tis then that Friendship's gentle hand
   May half our burden share;
'Tis then we fully understand
   The love to us they bear.

Oh! Love and Sympathy how dear
   To those bow'd down with care;
Thy angel-face dispels our fear,
   Makes hearts feel light as air.

Though Ophir's wealth were wholly mine,
   All jewels rich and rare,
For love of friends I yet would pine,
   And find my treasure there.

Our first experience at birth
   Was sympathy and love,
And when at last we leave this earth
   We'll find its Source above.

THE HAPPY HEART.

THE happy heart is a fount of joy,
    A bubbling spring of pleasure,
'Tis a source of constant sweet employ,
    A never-failing treasure!
Ready to smile with the flowers of Spring,
    Or sing with the birds of air;
In Nature's praise aye willing to sing,
    Finds happiness ev'rywhere.

The happy heart is so full of love
    That it speaks in every tone,
And the eyes of love, like stars above.
    Hath a glory all their own!
Like a beacon-light, in Grief's dark night,
    We long for the happy heart,
To shed o'er our pathway, calm and bright,
    A light that may not depart.

The happy heart is a gift from Heaven
    Above all treasure or gold,
Alike to the rich or poor 'tis given,
    It cannot be bought or sold!
The happy heart is the home of love,
    A solace for every woe;
Let us cherish this gift from above,
    As we seek our peace below.

THE OLD YEAR AND THE NEW.

LISTEN to the midnight bell,
Tolling out the old year's knell,
O'er our hearts there comes a spell
Such as when we say—"*Farewell!*"
As we ponder o'er the past,
Eyes are dim and overcast,
Silent falls full many a tear
As we part with thee—Old Year!

Seasons come and seasons go,
Summer's flowers and Winter's snow,
Like the ocean's ebb and flow,—
Joy and pain, and weal and woe!
Birthday greetings—glad and gay—
Wedded hearts were linked for aye,
Not a churchyard but a mound
Tells what reaper Death has found.

Yet we welcome thee, New Year,
And approach thee without fear,
Though we know not what may be
Portion'd out for us in thee;
Let us hope, and watch, and pray,
Growing wiser day by day;
Learning lessons from the past,
As this year may be *our* last!

Though the Old Year now must go,
Shrouded in a sheet of snow!
May the snow an emblem be
Of the New Year's purity!
As our footsteps in the snow
Show the path we wish to go,
May each day our record be—
Coming nearer, God, to Thee!

THE VOYAGE OF LIFE.

OH, life is like the ocean wide,
   With constant ebb and flow ;
And we the ships upon its tide,
   A-sailing to and fro ;
Each steering for some lovely isle
   Beyond the setting sun,
Hope on our pathway seems to smile,
   As on life's course we run.

Some ships sail well from first to last,
   With fair winds all the way,
At last their anchorage is cast
   Within some tranquil bay ;
While other scarcely leave the shore
   Ere dark clouds hover nigh,
And loud the angry tempests roar,
   Rude lightnings rend the sky.

But let us trim our sails aright,
   No storms shall overwhelm,
If we are brave and do the right,
   Let Faith direct our helm ;
We'll ride the waves, though mountains high,
   And sing our triumph-song,
Until we see the haven nigh
   To which our ships belong !

THE BITTER OR THE SWEET.

THE bitter or the sweet of life
   Is often ours to choose,
Sweet love is antidote to strife—
   The bitter, then, refuse.

Let not the angry word be said,
   At home, at work, or play;
Like waters pure from fountain-head
   Let smiles cheer up thy way.

Let Mara's bitter waters flow
   Alone on deserts wild;
On life's highway, whereon we go,
   Let looks and words be mild.

Let wreaths of smiles chase every frown
   From God's own image fair;
Then friendship's loving hands shall crown
   Thy head with blessings rare.

Now, all along life's rugged way
   Let flowers displace the thorn,
And grief and care shall flee away
   From hearts that erst were torn!

THE "DEAD-BEAT."*

LET'S beware of "the man (?)" who scorns
  to work,
Yet dare not refrain from eating!
In the core of his heart doth meanness lurk,
  In spite of his bland, fair greeting!

He may talk and look like " a gentleman,"
  And dress in the height of fashion;
He'll " run on credit " wherever he can,
  If " dunn'd "—gets into a passion!

He will oft-times talk of religion, too,
  And pray with seeming devotion;
He may go to church, yet pay for a pew—
  Of that he ne'er had a notion!

He carries his head like an English lord,
  Though he sometimes tastes of hunger!
He will eat at the widow's frugal board,
  And " skip " when she " trusts " no longer!

---

* " Dead-beat."—A well-known American phrase to denote one who is too lazy to work—a loafer!

His heart is devoid of affection dear,—
   He'd live off his poor old mother !
And will "sponge" on his friends both far and near,
   Claiming each one for a brother !

Oh ! out on the man with a heart of stone,
   Who knows not the pleasure of giving ;
Who will whimper, and whine, and beg, and groan—
   " That the world owes him a living !"

He who " will not work " should not dare to eat
   The bread of another's earning ;
For rather a thousand times sweep the street,
   Thereby independence learning !

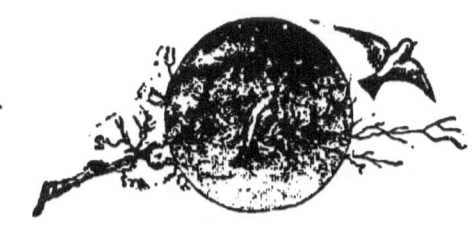

THE "EIGHT-HOUR" MOVEMENT.

LET the toilers have more leisure,
　　Listen to their urgent call,
Gain is not the only treasure,
　　Liberty is sweet to all;
Why should lives be spent in labour,
　　Early morn till darkness fall?
When, alas! a needy neighbour
　　Hath no work to do at all!

Why this labour agitation
　　All along the busy line?
'Tis the groaning of the nation—
　　Toilers feel they must combine;
Ere their rights have legislation,
　　Ere their wants shall have redress,
They must band in combination—
　　Ask their rights—and take no less!

Shorten, then, the hours of toiling,
　　Thus make work for idle men;
Cease this constant, weary moiling:
　　EIGHT hours work instead of TEN!
Justice doth exalt a nation,
　　Right is might, and truth shall stand,
Health is wealth in every station,
　　God shall prosper such a land!

THE BROTHERHOOD OF MAN.

OUR Father—God, His children—we,
No matter where our birthplace be—
'Mid Arctic snows, or torrid clime,
One family since the first of time!

We should not bind our fellow-man,
Though he be yellow, black, or tan;
Or seek to keep him trodden down
By haughty sneer, or cruel frown.

A mother's love, like that of Heav'n,
Alike to all her sons is giv'n,—
All men are free as God's pure air,
And all alike His image bear.

Far better we should ever try
To ease the load, or soothe the sigh;
Each other's burdens kindly bear,
Each other's joys or sorrows share!

How can we pray to God above,
And daily seek His care and love,
Unless our hearts for others' woe
With sympathetic love o'erflow?

YACHTING SONG.

SEE the " white caps " dance o'er the sparkling
    bay,
With a fresh strong breeze from the West;
Let us weigh the anchor and sail away,
    For our joy is the wave's white crest!

    CHORUS—
        Oh, ho! yah, ho! away we go,
           Like a gull o'er the bounding wave!
        With sails trim set from stern to bow—
           Yachting is the sport of the brave!

Let us sing the songs of the brave and free
    As we merrily glide along,
And waken the echoes along our lee
    While we carol our yachting song!

    CHORUS—" Oh, ho! yah, ho! away we go," &c.

As we leave the bay for the open lake
    Our hearts seem to swell with the tide,
Yet no fear have we though the billows break
    O'er our craft on the windward side!

    CHORUS—" Oh, ho! yah, ho! away we go," &c.

We seek no danger, yet we fear no fate,
    As we bend to the squall or gale;
And are happy as kings who ride in state,
    While we spread every inch of sail!

    CHORUS—" Oh, ho! yah, ho! away we go," &c.

THE BATTLE OF LIFE.

NOT where deadly bullets rattle
    Is the only hero-ground,
Nor upon the field of battle
    Are the most of heroes found ;
There are lives pure, noble and great,
    Yet we never hear their name,
Martyrs to duty—yet their fate
    Illumes not the page of fame !

In the daily struggle for bread
    There are scenes of direst woe,
The aching heart and throbbing head
    Doth company keep, we know ;
Life's great battle goes bravely on,—
    We hear but a smothered sigh,
The cross is kiss'd—the crown is won—
    As the vanquish'd heroes die !

Labor's pay is meagre and scant,
    The poor are but slaves to wealth ;
The hardest wrought know most of want,—
    May starve when broken in health ;
Dives still looks at the palace gate
    Where Lazarus moaning lies,
Nor seeks to ease his brother's fate—
    Through neglect and want he dies !

MISCELLANEOUS.

Oh! there are lives so fraught with grief
    And the sum of human woe,
In sleep alone is found relief
    From the cares that overflow;
Yet on they plod from day to day,
    Treading the Slough of Despond,
Hoping 'gainst hope—but to give way
    To the aching void beyond!

Oh! for the heaven beyond earth's cares,
    The love that dispels our fears,
God's answer to our fervent prayers
    And the Hand that wipes all tears;
The more of trial on earth we know
    The greater our joy in heaven,
Our empty hearts shall then o'erflow—
    The crown for the cross be given!

HIS ONLY PAIR OF PANTS.

Come, shed your pants this very minnit,
Until I put some stitches in it !
    Boys will be boys,
      No matter how ;
    An' as for noise,
      Losh ! what a row
They do kick up from morn' till night,
An' tease, an' squeeze, an' quarr'l, an' fight
    An' that's the way,
    'Most every day,
Your pants at knees and seat are bursted,
Tho' made o' strongest kind o' worsted !
    If they were made,
    As oft I've said,
Of half-inch, solid, well-tann'd leather,
I'm sure I don't know if they'd weather
    Such sad abuse,
    An' constant use,
An' hold your restless limbs together
Without the 'tention o' your mither !

HIS ONLY PAIR OF PANTS.

COME here, you little rag-a-muffin!
I'll give your ears a right good cuffin'!
 I do declare,
 Your only pair
Are torn again, an' fit for nuffin'
But nails, an' twine, an' marbles' stuffin'!
 Your nut-brown knees,
 By climbin' trees,
Have made some rents as big's a muffin,
An' yet you say, "*It's done by nuthin'!*"

Come, shed your pants this very minnit,
Until I put some stitches in it!
 Boys will be boys,
  No matter how;
 An' as for noise,
  . Losh! what a row
They do kick up from morn' till night,
An' tease, an' squeeze, an' quarr'l an' fight!
 An' that's the way,
 'Most every day,
Your pants at knees and seat are bursted,
Tho' made o' strongest kind o' worsted!
 If they were made,
 As oft I've said,
Of half-inch, solid, well-tann'd leather,
I'm sure I don't know if they'd weather
 Such sad abuse,
 An' constant use,
An' hold your restless limbs together
Without the 'tention o' your mither!

See, there, my stars! your pants are patch'd,
With scarce an inch o' cloth that's match'd!
     Now, put them on,
     An' get to school,
     But, mind you, John,
     I've made a rule :—
If you come back like that again,
An' from your climbin' don't refrain,
     I'll turn you oot,
     Without a suit,
To wander in the wind and rain,
An' dare you to come back again,
     An' then, my lad,
     You will be glad
To take more pains to save your knees,
When climbin' fences, posts, and trees,
An' me the 'tendin' o' your wants,
To patch your " only pair o' pants !"

WHAT SHALL I SING?

SING a merry, happy lay,
   Bright as Summer's golden day,
When the hours fly swift away,
   Oh! sing of these to me!

Sing of birds, and bees, and flowers,
Sing of Flora's lovely bowers,
Sing of early childhood's hours,
   Oh! sing of these to me!

Sing the songs that touch the heart,
Causing tears of joy to start,—
Sing of friends that never part,
   Oh! sing of these to me!

Wooing like the gentle dove,
Sing of happiness and love,
Sing of brighter joys above
   Oh! sing of these to me!

Sing of these, and I shall sing,
As if borne on angel's wing
To the presence of the King,
   There evermore to be!

TODDLIN' HAME!

 BONNIE sicht it is to see
    A bairnie " toddlin hame,"
Wi' ootstretched airms an' muckle glee,
    It lisps its faither's name!

In a guid sense we're a' like weans,
    Toddlin' heavenward hame !
Stap clear o' a' life's stum'lin stanes
    As ye gang " toddlin' hame ! "

Wale oot the flowers alang life's way—
    Dae richt, an' daur the blame,
Mak' life be as a simmer's day—
    Year in, year oot, the same !

Some folks hae joy frae morn' to nicht,
    Cheerily " toddlin' hame ; "
'Mang hope, an' happiness, an' licht,
    They wale their fitstaps hame !

Ithers seem fash'd wi' doots an' pain,
 As they gang hirplin' hame!
Like some wee, puir, forsaken wean,
 That's tint its faither's name!

Some reach their hame afore midday,
 Whan' mornin' glories bloom;
Some tread a lang and thorny way
 Afore they reach the tomb!

Oor Faither waits ayont life's stream,
 An' welcomes a' the same;
The love-licht in His e'e doth gleam
 To see us "toddlin' hame!"

MY MITHER'S GRAVE.

I STAN' beside the cauld head-stane,
   An' wat it wi' my tears ;
An' whisper, "*Mither, here's your wean
   You hav'na' seen for years!*"
Whan last I saw your dear, sweet face,
   An' heard your kindly tone,
I little thought that this dread place
   So soon would claim its own.

I plann'd to tak' you ower the sea
   To comfort an' to ease,
Whaur you could end your days wi' me,
   An' dae maist as you please ;
But, ah ! the Lord had ither plans,
   An' sent for you Himsel' ;
His ways are no' aye like to man's,
   Yet does He a' things well !

But, though you cannot come to me,
　I yet shall gang to you,
When death shall set my spirit free
　I'll mount the starry blue,
Where grief an' partings are no more
　Nor Death, nor any pain,
You'll welcome me on Canaan's shore,
　We'll never pairt again!

Farewell! most sacred spot to me,
　My dear auld mither's grave,
I'll think o' thee when ower the sea,
　Ayont Atlantic's wave;
Our graves may yet be far apart,
　Our spirits joined shall be,
There's aye a green spot in my heart,
　My mither dear, for thee!

OUR FAITHER ABUNE.

THE licht o' the mornin' should see us a-steer
    The wark o' the day to begin,
Bit afore we commence our hearts it wad cheer
    To speak to our Faither abune;
Each day has its cares, an' its trials, an' toil,
    Its pleasures, its praise, an' its blame;
As dew to the grass, or as rain to the soil—
    God's blessin' afore we lea' hame!

Devotion uplifts us on wings o' the dove,
    An' sets a' our heart in a flame,
To feel that our Faither is watchin' above
    An' kens us each ane by our name!
It maks us feel strong for the battle o' life,
    An' gies us baith courage an' vim,
To fight wi' temptation, an' win in the strife,
    Prayer brings us aye nearer to Him!

An' when we come hame, ere we gang to oor bed,
    Oor prayers to forget is a shame,
For in His Guid Book how aften 'tis said:
    " I loe them that ca' on My name!"
" The secret o' God is wi' them that Him fear,"
    He'll shield them frae a' Satan's blame;
An' whan we lie doon for to dee He'll be near
    To bring His ain bairnies a' hame!

MISCELLANEOUS.

"IS THIS LIFE WORTH LIVING?"

"IS this life worth living?" you ask;
   Perhaps not—to those who repine,
And murmur at life's daily task,
   Commencing each day with a whine!

The cowards who fret at their lot,
   And listlessly pass time away,
Are not worth the " six-by-three plot,"
   Or the shroud that'll wrap their dead clay!

Yes, life is worth living! thank God!
   To those who are honest and true;
Who smile at misfortune, and plod
   Till success doth crown them anew!

Oh! life is God's blessing to man,
   Though ever so humble our lot;
Let each do the good that he can,—
   'Tis better to " wear out " than rot!

Then, let not a murmur be heard,
   Let duty encompass each hour;
Thank God for the life that is spar'd,—
   In labor is honor and power!

WHEN LOVE IS KING!

LOVE'S youthfu' years are swift an' sweet,
   An' fu' o' hope sae cheerie, O!
Whan heart wi' heart in union meet
   O' love they never wearie, O!
This life to them is naught but bliss,
   To each they're a' that's dearie, O!
Whan vows are answer'd wi' a kiss
   How can this life be drearie, O?

CHORUS,—
      Noo, dinna fash yer head ava',
         Wi' cares an' worries drearie, O!
      Whan Love is king just mind his law,
         O' that you'll never wearie, O!

Bind hearts wi' Love sae firm an' fast,
   Nae bands like His can tether, O!
Love's sunnie smiles through life should last,
   And brave life's wintry weather, O!
Our riper years shall fruitful be,
   An' happy a'thegither, O!
It's time enough to wish to dee
   When ower us grows the heather, O!

CHORUS,—
      Noo, dinna fash yer head ava'!
         Wi' cares an' worries drearie, O!
      Whan Love is king just mind his law,
         O' that you'll never wearie, O!

TOBOGGANING SONG.

'TIS "Hurrah! hurrah!" and away they go,
Like an avalanche o'er the crispy snow !
With a rush and a bound they clear the ground,
While the snow, like spray, dashes all around !
    They think not of death,
    Yet they hold their breath,—
Now in a hollow !—now cresting a hill !—
There, guiding the craft to prevent " a spill ! "
See ! the fresh warm blood to their faces rush,
As they peep from their robes with roses' blush !
    In the clear moonlight,
    What a happy sight,—
As the maiden clings with a tender fear
To the kind loving arm that holds her near !
Through the clear cold air of the frosty night
The twinkling stars seem to dance with delight !
    With speed of the wind—
    Leaving all behind—
They rush to the plain with a shout of glee,
As merry and happy as hearts could be !

THE GOLDEN RULE.

SPEAK a kind word when you can,
   Kind words cost but little,
This is far the better plan,
   Human hearts are brittle.

Life is all too short for strife,
   Peace and love are golden ;
For they serve to lengthen life,
   So say sages olden !

Let us lend a helping hand
   To each weary brother,
Are we not a pilgrim band
   Bound to one another ?

Our reward shall greater be
   When we get to heaven,
If to duty faithfully
   We have daily striven !

Life to us is like a school
   Where our good behaviour
Should be as " the Golden Rule "
   Taught us by our Saviour :—

" Do to others as you would
   That they should do to you ;"
Then shall we be truly good,
   And life's regrets be few !

TO-MORROW!

LIFE'S lessons from the past we borrow,—
To-day is ours, but not to-morrow;
Then, smile to-day, leave care and sorrow
One day a-head, say—" *Yes, to-morrow !*"

Make friends to-day for use to-morrow,
They'll help to drive away dull sorrow;
And from their friendship sweetness borrow
To bless each day and crown each morrow.

Make love to-day!—make more to-morrow!
You'll have to spare when others borrow!
'Twill be an antidote to sorrow
Should it perchance arise—to-morrow!

" To-morrow never comes," but each "to-day,"
Links out life's chain from cradle to decay!

SABBATH CHIMES.

DINGLE, dingle, dong!
   Hear the happy song:
     Come away,
     Sabbath day,
Join the holy throng.

Come, both old and young,
Come, the weak or strong,
     Dingle dong!
     Happy song,
Cheering us along.

Children, young and fair,
Seeking God in prayer,
     Voices raise,
     In His praise,
Feeling God is there.

Plainly all may see,
Happy hearts have we,
     God above,
     Full of love,
Keep us near to Thee!

THE BONNIE ARRAN HILLS!

As seen on board of an ocean steamer by the writer, a native of Scotland, when returning from a prolonged absence in America.

AS I approach thee, lovely Clyde,
  My heart wi' rapture thrills,
My longing eyes behold wi' pride
  The bonnie Arran hills;
The graceful bend o' Brodick Bay
  Calls back the scenes o' yore,
When many a happy summer's day
  Was spent upon thy shore?

CHORUS—
    Oh, Arran hills! dear Arran hills!
      I've long'd sae aft to see;
    Wi' native pride, my bosom thrills,
      Weel may I sing o' thee!

And there, defying change o' Time,
  Stan's clear against the sky,
The mountain-tap I used to climb,
  Dear auld Goat Fell sae high;
Glen Sannox nestles at thy fit—
  The sight my rapture wins—
An' roon thy sides the swallows flit,
  'Mang heather, flowers, and whins!

CHORUS—
    Oh, Arran hills! dear Arran hills!
      I've lang'd sae aft to see;
    Wi' native pride, my bosom thrills,
      Weel may I sing o' thee!

The bonnie Arran hills for me
  Wi' sunlit taps o' glory,
Fit emblem o' the brave an' free
  O' ancient Scottish story!
When far frae thee o'er ocean wide,
  Fond memories come to cheer me,
I'll sing o' thee wi' loyal pride,
  An' wish I was but near thee!

Chorus—
          Oh, Arran hills! dear Arran hills!
            I've long'd sae aft to see;
          Wi' native pride my bosom thrills,
            Weel may I sing o' thee!

THE SUNDAY-SCHOOL INFANT CLASS.

SIXTY little smiling faces,
All in their accustom'd places;
Each a happy household's treasure,
Teaching them a perfect pleasure.

Sixty pair of eyes, whose gladness
Shews no trace of care or sadness,
Are fix'd on me with glances bright,
Like twinkling orbs of purest light.

Sixty voices in a chorus:
"*Childhood's years are passing o'er us;*"
May those years to God be given,
Walking in the way to Heaven.

Hopeful hearts are rais'd in pray'r,
Craving God's peculiar care;
Waiting for the children's blessing,
Faith and love their hearts possessing.

Childish words, brimful of trust:
"*Jesus, Thou canst make us just,*"
May we now and ever share
In our Father's watchful care."

How they listen to the story
Of redeeming love and glory:
That Jesus took the sinner's place,
In boundless love and matchless grace.

MISCELLANEOUS.

Simple words and illustration,
Suited to their humble station;
"Line upon line" they learn to know
The Word of God, and wiser grow.

Their minds, thus stor'd with heavenly truth,
Will fence them from the snares of youth,
And thus a safe foundation lay
To lead them through life's rugged way.

Oh, blessed are the children dear
Who love the Lord, and in His fear
Do walk in His most holy way
That leads to everlasting day!

And blessed is the teacher's part,
To educate the infant heart;
A Saviour's love to them unfold,
Truths ever new and never old!

THE ABSENT SUNDAY-SCHOOL TEACHER.

OH! children dear,
   She is not here,
Your teacher loving and true;
   But gone above,
   Where all is love,
Waiting and watching for you.

   For you her tears,
   And pray'rs, and fears,
Will not have been spent in vain;
   If lessons taught
   Are not forgot,
You shall meet with her again!

   In that bright land,
   At God's right hand,
Where Jesus shall claim His own,—
   With smiling face,
   Appoint a place
Around His glorious throne.

   Oh! happy land,
   Thrice happy band,
Beside the shining river;
   In Jesus' praise
   Your voices raise
In songs that last for ever!

MISCELLANEOUS.

THE "LOVES" OF AN INFANT-CLASS SCHOLAR.

I love to hear the school-bell ring,
I love to hear the children sing;
I love to see the house of pray'r,
I love to *know* that God is there.

I love to see my teacher's face,
All beaming with a heavenly grace;
I love to make my teacher glad,
When naughty children make her sad.

I love to read my Bible true,
I love my Father's will to do;
I love to *feel* my sins forgiv'n,
I love to think of God and Heav'n.

I love to learn the heavenly way,
In Sabbath-school—on Sabbath day;
I love to bring my playmates there,
I love my lessons to prepare.

I love my mother—oh, so dear!
I love my father's heart to cheer;
I love my brothers, kind and true,
I love my own dear sisters too.

I love to think of Jesus mild,
And how He loves a little child ;
I love to know that " GOD IS LOVE,"
And smiles on me from Heav'n above.

I love to think that when I die
God waits for me beyond the sky ;
And when I reach that " happy land,"
I'll walk with Jesus hand-in-hand !

THE AFRICAN SLAVE TRADE.

OH ! fathers and mothers,
   Oh ! sisters and brothers,
Who freedom and liberty claim,—
   There are dark spots on earth
   Where, as yet, Freedom's birth
Is known to its sons but in name !

   There's a horrible trade,
   In man, woman, and maid,
Carried on by demons of earth,—
   Where, for base love of gold,
   The poor Negro is sold,
And borne from the land of their birth !

Hark! a shriek—shrill and wild!
At the death of her child
All mangled, and bleeding, and torn :
'Tis a mother's despair
That has just rent the air—
A slave to the market she's borne!

What a depleted host,
As they march to the coast,
Chain'd, halter'd, and whipp'd as they go ;
This accursed slave-trade
Is like Death's cavalcade,
Let free nations deal out its death-blow!

They are helpless and weak,
And their cries to us speak
Of anguish, and sorrow, and pain ;
Oh! our God shall look down
On our ease with a frown,
If their cry for our help is vain!

Oh! ye nations of light,
Arise in your might,
This "human-flesh traffic" destroy ;
Till that down-trodden race,
Shall at last take their place,
'Mong nations of earth with great joy!

THE NURSERY CLOCK.

TICK, tickaty, tickaty tock,
I'm only the nursery clock,
   By night and by day,
   I'm wagging away,
Tick, tickaty, tickaty tock !

How I love when the children play
In the nursery day by day,
   I can't leave my place,
   Yet know each wee face,—
Tick sadly when they go away !

When some one is sick in the house,
I "tick-tick" as quiet as a mouse ;
   The girls and the boys
   Make play without noise,—
There's quietness all over the house !

One night in the year I know well,
The secret I'm going to tell:—
   When Santa Claus comes,
   With toys, dolls, and drums,
I tick then as loud as a bell !

I want all the children to hear,
But none of them ever come near,
   So quiet do they keep
   They must be asleep
'Twill never be morning I fear !

I " tick-tick " as fast as I can,
Sixty ticks each minute my plan ;
   I'm happy at last,—
   Wee feet running fast,
Quick into my room they all ran !

When Mamma and Pa comes to see
The reason of all this great glee,
   I join in the fun
   Of Christmas begun,
A smile on my face you might see !

SKATING.

I.

OH! for the blue sky, bright and clear,
And the sunshine all around;
With gay companions hovering near,
Skimming o'er the crystal ground!
  Happy are we,
  So glad and free,
  Racing!—Chasing!
  Away we go,
  O'er ice and snow,
  Sliding!—Gliding!
  Whirling around
  The giddy ground,
  Madly!—Gladly!
Scudding along before the wind,
No thought of care have we;
Leaving the laggards all behind—
Oh! skating's the sport for me!

II.

Oh! for the hand of one I love
To guide o'er the glassy sea;
And press the tiny snow-white glove,
That struggles not to be free!
  Her eyes of love,
  Like stars above,
  Their light—Makes night
  Seem bright as day!
  Hours fly away
  Lightly!—Brightly!
  In merry fun,
  We laughing run,
  Tripping!—Skipping!
Then homeward wend our moonlit way,
Two pairs of skates I carry!—
And beg of her to name the day
When skaters TWO may marry!

JOHN THREE-SIXTEEN!

"For God so loved the world, that He gave His only begotten Son, that whosoever believeth in Him should not perish, but have everlasting life."—*John iii. 16.*

A LITTLE boy, some eight years old,—
   A friendless orphan waif—
One evening, shiver'd in the cold,
   And look'd for shelter safe ;
But as he tried each snug retreat,
   By police was found out,
And often he was cuff'd and beat,
   And told to " move about ! "

He crept along the cheerless street,
   His clothes were thin and wet,
No shoes or stockings on his feet,
   No friendly soul he met.
But one—a tender, kindly man—
   Who saw his sorry plight,
And thought upon a lucky plan
   To shelter him that night.

" My boy ! " the stranger kindly said,
   In tones that touch'd his heart,
" I'll tell you where to get a bed
   If you will act your part :
Just go to number ten Blank street,
   A home for friendless boys,
There you will find a snug retreat,—
   Be good—and make no noise ! "

"You bet, I'll only be too glad
  To take your kind advice!"
And eager lit were eyes once sad
  At thought of home so nice;
He quickly turned his steps to go
  To number ten Blank street,
"But," said the stranger, "you must know
  The 'key' to that retreat!

"Now, just when you get there, my boy,
  You'll give your name, I ween,
They'll welcome you with love and joy,
  Say—'I'm John Three-sixteen!'"
He almost ran, though cold and wet,
  As oft before he'd been;
And mutter'd oft—lest he'd forget—
  "I'm John—John Three-sixteen!"

He reached the place, and rang the bell,
  The matron got a fright!
"Who that can be I cannot tell
  At such a time of night!"
She open'd carefully the door,
  And there the waif was seen;
She ask'd if he'd been there before—
  "No, I'm John Three-sixteen!"

"'John Three-sixteen!' that sounds so queer,
  But I've heard that before,—
Step out the rain and come in here,
  And I will shut the door;
John Three-sixteen! you're welcome here,
  My little homeless one;
'For God so loved the world,' my dear,
  'That He gave up His Son!'"

WHEN JESUS WAS AWAY.

A TRUE INCIDENT.

A LITTLE girl, just four years old,
 Lay on her dying bed,
Her silken tresses shone like gold—
 Seem'd halo round her head;
The early morning sun peep'd in
 And lit her pale sweet face—
So angel-like—no trace of sin
 Could mar that holy place!

She ope'd her eyes and look'd around,
 Smil'd sweetly on her Pa,
And said, in tones of softest sound,
 " I want to speak to Ma;
Oh! I had such a lovely dream,
 I thought I was in heaven!"
O'er all her face there shone a gleam,
 To angels only given!

" Oh! heaven is such a pretty place,
 With streets of shining gold,
And Jesus seem'd to know my face,
 His arms did me enfold;
I felt so happy, Mamma, dear,
 The angels seem'd so too,
I did not have the slightest fear,
 Though all was strange and new!"

MISCELLANEOUS.

"And then I woke, yet still I'm here,
    So glad to be with you,
But yet I love those angels dear,
    Beyond the skies so blue !
How lone the angels must have been,
    When Jesus was away !
How good He was to bear our sin,
    I feel it more to-day !"

A few short days of weary pain
    Her dream was realized,
She went to view those scenes again—
    To Jesus whom she priz'd ;
Engrav'd on stone may now be seen,
    Above her lifeless clay :
" *How lone the angels must have been,*
    When Jesus was away !"

A lesson here for us within
    This simple little lay,
How lonely must we all have been
    Had Jesus stay'd away !
Oh, let us thank Him day and night
    For Calvary's sacrifice,
And wait His call to mansions bright,—
    To God and Paradise !

THE DRUNKARD!

" ALL RIGHT !" he cried aloud, "*All right !*"
 But wiser people said : " He's tight!"
And he seem'd "spoiling for a fight!"
  Made mad through cursed drink.

"*All right !*" he said, as reeling home,
With bloodshot eyes and mouth all foam,
All o'er the side-walk he doth roam,—
  Blind drunk through greed of drink!

"*All right !*" he stumbl'd, swore, and fell,
One awful word he said—'twas "*Hell !*"
Then, surely, he was 'neath its spell,—
  Led by the demon—Drink!

Though oft he slipp'd upon the road,
He reach'd at last his poor abode,
There sank he on the floor—a load
  Scarce human—craz'd by drink!

His children fled from him in fear,
His wife, heart-broken, dropt a tear,
His very dog it came not near,—
  All fear'd him when in drink!

All's wrong !—and yet he says, " *All right !* "
Tho' all his future's dark as night,
Upon his home there seems a blight,—
  The consequence of drink!

These are thy fruits, oh, Upas-tree!
Death's fatal draught's distill'd by thee,
Thy victims never can be free,
  If lur'd by thee to drink!

MISCELLANEOUS.

Oh, God in Heaven, hear the prayer
Of mothers, wives, and children fair,
For lov'd ones driven to despair,—
  " *God save them from strong drink !* "

God haste the day when this fair land
Shall Prohibition's law demand,—
When men and women show their hand
  By voting 'gainst strong drink!

SCARBORO' HEIGHTS.

WHERE Lake Ontario's broad expanse
    Lies spread before me like a sea,
There do I stand as in a trance
    And view a scene that's sweet to me!

CHORUS.
    Oh! Scarboro' heights, I love thee well,
      Thy flowery dells are dear to me ;
    'Twas there I met thee, darling Nell,
      And vow'd I ne'er would part from thee.

We roam'd the woods in search of flowers,
    And found them plenty, fair, and free ;
Thus pass'd Love's sunny, golden hours,
    The fairest flower I found was thee !—CHORUS.

The silver moon rose from the Lake,
    The fading sunset grand to see,
A golden ring for Love's sweet sake
    Was there and then bestowed on thee.—CHORUS.

The years may come, the years may go,
    But mem'ries dear shall never fade,
While blue Ontario's waters flow
    We'll ne'er forget the vows we made.—CHORUS.

A SCOTCH SURPRISE PARTY.

AE nicht I sat my lee-some lain,
 Beside the big ha' stove,
A-dreamin' ower an' ower again
 O' folk an' scenes I love ;
In thocht I cross'd the big saut sea,
 An' smelt the caller air
O' bonnie Scotland, dear to me,
 My native lan' sae fair !

Guid bless my heart ! what's that I hear ?
 The strains o' " Tullochgorum ! "
Some Heilan' laddies maun be near,
 Guid feith I'll jine their quorum !
I took my bonnet frae the wa',
 An' roun' me drew my plaidie,
Then, briskly stapit frae the ha'
 Said—" Lads, I'll walk beside ye ! "

We march'd a' up an' doon the toon,
 The chanter gaed a-hummin' ;
The piper noo had changed his tune :—
 " The Campbells are a-comin' ! "
It made me walk sae smart an' vain,
 I couldna' speak my feelin's,—
It seem'd to me like hame again,
 An' I were in the Hielan's !

PATRIOTIC.

We marched into a great big ha',
    Like colts we a' got prancin',
Sinc lads an' lassies ane an' a'
    Pair'd oot an' fell a-dancin' !
It was a happy nicht to me,
    Wi' fun an' daffin' cheerie ;
I'll mind it till the day I dee,
    We never seem'd to wearie !

We a' join'd hands an' made a ring,
    I'lk jo link'd to his dearie,
An' then we a' began to sing :—
    " For a' lang syne," fu' cheerie !
'Twas then amang the wee sma' hours,
    The snaw was fa'in' rarely :
Ilk tartan plaid wrapt twa Scotch flowers,—
    The piper played—" Prince Charlie !"

BURIED IN HER CRADLE.

"The cherry-wood cradle in which Mrs. Ruth Hall, of Willingford, Connecticut, was rocked in when a baby, has, by her own special request, been made into a coffin for that good lady."—*American Exchange.*

SHE had cross'd the line of three-score and ten,
    For her last birthday was seventy-four,
Yet she thought of her childhood's days, and when,
    As a babe, she was rock'd to sleep once more!
And it seem'd to soothe her—the very thought
    That she still had the cradle used of yore,
So out from the lumber-room it was brought,
    And she playfully rock'd it on the floor!

The "style" of this cradle was "out of date"—
    Nigh a hundred years had it service seen—
It was deep and wide, and its size was great,
    As the cribs of the olden time have been!
But many a handsome babe had slept there,
    As cosy and warm as infant could be;
While mothers had rocked, oft a fervent prayer
    Had been breath'd beside it on bended knee!

See! a big tear drops from her sad blue eye,
   As she thinks of the children once she bore,
Who slept in that cradle in years gone by,
   But now " rest in peace " on the other shore !
A glow of affection swept over her heart,
   As she ponder'd on years of motherly care,
And she felt as if she never could part
   With that cherry-wood cradle standing there !

She look'd on the cradle and feebly said :
   " We both have grown old together, you see,
I wish from my heart that when I am dead,
   A coffin from this might be made for me ;
I think I could rest more peacefully there,
   The long sleep of death would be sweet to me ;
And ' mother ' would wake me in heaven so fair
   With kisses and smiles as it used to be ! "

Her wish was granted ; her coffin was made
   From the cherry-wood crib that used to be ;
And in it a pillow of down was laid,
   For the head from worry and care set free !
There she looked so calm, and sweet, and still,—
   'Mong the flowers and lilies her children brought ;
She seemed so content, for she had her will,—
   To sleep in her cherry-wood cradle cot !

MORTGAGING THE HOMESTEAD.

Composed on seeing an artistic painting on the above subject, by G. A. Reid, R. C. A., Toronto, on exhibition in a shop-window on Yonge Street, Toronto, Canada.

DON'T mortgage the homestead, my brother,
  'Tis the greatest mistake of your life,
Take courage, and help one another,
  For the sake of your children and wife;
Far better a crust in contentment
  Than a mortgage and well-buttered bread,
Don't risk a mortgagee's resentment,
  He may yet make you wish you were dead.

Oh, don't mortgage the homestead, my friend,
  Rather work like a slave and be free !
You will find this advice in the end
  Is the best that a friend could give thee;
Rise bright with the dawn of the morning,
  Let sweet hope cheer you on till the eve,
List' not to the world's proud scorning,
  Let them see that in God you believe.

Don't mortgage your homestead, my neighbour,
   Hark! the voice of your own loving wife :—
"We now must dispense with hir'd labor,
   Let us pull well together through life ;
Our children will soon be a help, dear,
   We'll have no heavy mortgage to pay,
Let us leave well alone, never fear,
   I will help you by night and by day!"

Don't mortgage your homestead, my brother.
   Do not risk all the savings of years,
And leave in the hands of another
   What has cost you toil, worry, and tears ;—
Be a man!—your wife will adore you,
   Ne'er give up while you've courage and health,
You will find this good motto is true :
   'Tis the diligent hand maketh wealth !

TO JOHN IMRIE.

From ALBERT E. S. SMYTHE, *Toronto.*

IMRIE, your lyrics pass the laws of kings
   Whose dread decrees but steeled the captive's
    heart;
Your home-taught lays a softer power impart,—
Love, joy, and peace, the might that mercy brings:
And, though your muse lack flight of angel's wings,
To walk and talk with men is no mean art,
   Strong in life's straits, secure against death's dart,
Attuned to truth, foreprizing hallowed things.
Not of the mockers, nor of those who make
   Love's sacrament a feasting, passion-spiced;
Not lucre-thralled, nor cankered with the ache
   Of envy; free of almsdeed honour-priced;
Not of the world; but humbly, for His sake,
   Striving the nobler manhood after Christ.

In answer to the above.

TO A BROTHER BARD.

DEAR brother bard, a tender chord
   Hath been unstrung by thee,
Thy " pen is mightier than the sword,"
   And it hath vanquish'd me!
Love is a power to conquer men,
   It knoweth not defeat,—
I am the captive of thy pen
   And worship at thy feet!

MISCELLANEOUS.

Thou hast a power I never knew
    To touch the inner heart,
A gift God giveth to the few
    Who choose the better part;
'Tis like the first glint of the morn
    That speaks the hopeful day,
You sing—for singing thou wast born—
    Thy songs shall ne'er decay!

To speak the fullness of the soul
    And sound it forth in songs,
To make the wounded spirit whole
    This art to few belongs;
I would not for the gold of earth
    Renounce this wealth of love,
That heart enjoys perpetual mirth,
    Attun'd to harps above!

Sing on! though humble be thy lot,
    Thy recompense is this,—
To cast a halo o'er each spot
    Where memory is bliss!
Each truth express'd is like a flower
    To cheer some drooping heart,
And cause them bless the heaven-born power
    That lent to thee such art!

"GOOD-BYE!"

"GOOD-BYE! good-bye!" what kindly words,
 As they fall on the parting ear,
Like the singing of summer birds,
 With their wonderful power to cheer;
  Their meaning true—
  " God-be-with-you!"
  With kiss and sigh—
  " Good-bye! good-bye!"

" Good-bye! good-bye!" means not " Farewell!"
 But a wish for our Father's care!
How sweet when hearts their fullness tell
 In the words of that loving prayer;
  " Good-bye! good-bye!"
  May God be nigh;
  The meaning true—
  " God-be-with-you!"

These words are sometimes idly said,
　Like passing sunbeams on the wall,
And on the heart fall cold and dead,
　'Tis then no fervent prayer at all,
　　　But plain—" Good-bye!"—
　　　A formal cry,
　　　No kiss nor sigh,
　　　Ah, friends!—why? why?

Remember, when you say—" Good-bye!'
　Life is uncertain, short, and fleet;
Then, let the love-light in your eye
　Show friendship's bond is strong and sweet
　　　Thus, hand-in-hand,
　　　Friends understand
　　　The meaning true—
　　　" God-be-with-you!"

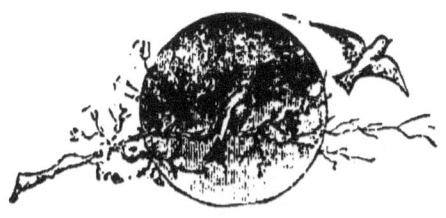

"FAREWELL!"

THE saddest word we ever hear,
Full-fraught with sorrow, hope, and fear,
The fount of many a bitter tear:
　Farewell! Farewell!

REFRAIN:　Farewell! Farewell!
　　Ah! who can tell
　　　What bitter tears,
　　　What hopes and fears,
　　Surround thy spell?
　　Sad word: "Farewell!"

As, branch by branch, the family tree
Is snapp'd and floated o'er life's sea,
How sad a parent's heart must be,
　To say: "Farewell!"

REFRAIN: "Farewell! Farewell!" etc.

How sad for loving friends to part
For distant scenes—so wide apart—
That mem'ries must suffice the heart
　That says: "Farewell!"

REFRAIN: "Farewell! Farewell!" etc.

MISCELLANEOUS.

How sad to hear the deep-toned bell
Ring out a dear friend's funeral knell,
And feel your very heart-strings swell
  To say: "Farewell!"

REFRAIN: "Farewell! Farewell!" etc.

When we have said our last "Farewell,"
And gone the ranks of heaven to swell,
Rejoice to know—Death breaks the spell—
  All's well! all's well!

REFRAIN: With God to dwell,
    No more, "Farewell!"
    No more sad tears!
    No doubts! no fears!
    Each tongue shall tell:
  "'Tis well! 'Tis well!"

FRAGMENTS FOR AUTOGRAPH ALBUMS.

A FEW short years
   Of hopes and fears,
And then we pass for ever,
   Where answer'd prayers
   Shall banish cares,
Beyond the shining river !

   Blest land above,
   Sweet home of love,
With joy we'll reach thy portals;
   'Mid angel throngs,
   Recite the songs
Sung by redeem'd immortals !

FRIENDSHIP.

THE friendship of the good and true
   Is more to me than gold,
And, while I welcome one that's new,
   I'll treasure well the old ;
Old friends are like the goodly tree
   Whose leafy branches throw
A grateful shelter over me
   When adverse winds may blow !

A BIRTHDAY WISH.

BIRTHDAY greetings now I send,
   Full of gladness, love, and joy,
May this year, my loving friend,
   Bring thee peace without alloy ;
Keep this token as a charm,
   Proof of Friendship ever dear,
Fain would I shield thee from harm
   All this happy golden year !

SACRED COMPOSITIONS.

Sacred Compositions.

A PRAYER.

LOWLY and prostrate,
 Kneeling before Thee,
Craving the spirit of prayer;
 Wretched and lonely,
 Seeking Thee only,
Leave me not now in despair.

Father of mercies,
 And God of all might,
Hear Thou the sigh of my heart;
 Groping through darkness,
 Yet seeking the light,
Pardon and peace now impart.

Oh! to be nothing,
 And Christ to be all,
Oh! to be ransomed by Thee;
 Saved from destruction
 And pow'r of the fall,
Through Jesus, who died for me.

Humbly I ask Thee,
 Jesus, my Saviour,
Bend Thou Thine ear to my cry;
 For strength and for grace
 While running life's race—
Lead Thou me on till I die!

AN ANXIOUS SOUL COMFORTED.

POOR erring soul! thou art not yet forsaken,
   A Father's loving heart still beats for thee;
Renounce the steps in sin which thou hast taken,
   And thou shalt have a pardon full and free.

Let not the sins of former days deter
   Thy heart from seeking after truth and God;
Thou shalt not seek in vain, do not defer,
   Fly to the Cross, and Christ shall ease thy load.

A Father's arms are opened to receive,
   A Saviour's blood was freely shed for thee;
Trust not thy erring self, in Him believe,
   Who bore thy sins upon the curséd tree.

No more in darkness shalt thou doubting tread,
   A brighter Light shall guide thee on thy way;
No more in sin shalt thou be blindly led,
   Nor in the paths of vice be found to stray.

Thy soul shall then in glorious measure feel
   The Spirit's power, which changes mind and will;
And thou shalt not be able to conceal
   The love which thy enraptur'd soul shall fill.

Then shalt thou grow in grace from day to day,
   And thus be fitted for the home above;
Till God shall call thy ransom'd soul away
   To swell the praises of His matchless love.

"COME UNTO ME!"

"Him that cometh unto Me, I will in no wise cast out."

COME! weary, fainting, contrite heart,
And bid thy doubts and fears depart,
Though tears of penitence may start
    From downcast eyes,—
Come! though your sins are crimson red,
For you a Saviour's blood was shed,
For you He bow'd His thorn-crown'd head,
    'Mid groans and sighs:
    Oh! Come! Come! Come!

Come! while God's Spirit pleads with power,
Come! linger not another hour,
Come! ere the clouds of doubt shall lower
    And mar thy sight;
Come! now, while yet 'tis call'd "To-day!"
Come! from the snares of sin away,
Come! ere thy feet have learn'd to stray
    From God and right:
    Oh! Come! Come! Come!

Come! in the attitude of prayer,
Come! cast on God your every care,
Come! all your wants and sins declare,
    God's mercy seek;
To thee the Comforter shall bring
"Peace!" that shall cause thy heart to sing;
Then to The Rock for ever cling,
    His praises speak:
    Oh! Come! Come! Come!

THE PREACHER'S WARNING.

REMEMBER, O youth! in thy early prime,
The God of thy fathers in olden time:
The Creator of heaven, and earth, and spheres,
With whom one day is as a thousand years;
While the years of man are as early grass,
To-day in health, but to-morrow doth pass
In natural course of decay away,
To mingle again with its mother—Clay!

Ere the evil days come and years draw nigh,
When pleasure and hope give way to a sigh;
And the eye whose lustre was clear and bright,
Gives forth but a dim and uncertain light;
And the step, once firm and lithe in the dance,
Be crippled, and weak, and slow to advance;
Oh! young man, beware, and remember now
Thy Creator—God, and thy father's vow!

Let faith and prayer like daily incense rise
To God above, beyond the starry skies;
Seek wisdom from on high as daily food,
Let not thy left hand mar thy right hand's good;
But grow in grace, and in the knowledge rare
Which maketh rich, and Christ's atonement share;
Then shall thy path be as the rising sun,
And God at last shall say—*Well done, well done!*

SACRED.

JESUS' LOVE.

OH, wondrous love! oh, matchless grace!
That Jesus took the sinner's place;
And left His heavenly home on high,
On earth to *live*, to *weep*, to *die*.

To live on earth that we might rise
To brighter scenes beyond the skies;
And dwell in mansions fair and bright,
'Mid endless glory, love, and light.

To weep, that we might sing for joy,
And all our ransom'd powers employ;
Our hearts and voices gladly raise
In happy songs of love and praise.

To die, that we might never die,
But live with Him in bliss on high;
And meet around that glorious throne,
Where Jesus gathers in His own.

The love of Jesus, like the sea,
Is rich and boundless, full and free;
No seeking soul need e'er despair,
Or fail to find a portion there.

THE BELIEVER'S REFUGE.

'TIS sweet to feel that God is near
    In times of trouble or distress,—
To quell the doubt, or calm the fear,
    To pardon, comfort, heal and bless.

When all around is dark and drear,
    And sorrow shades the brow with care,
How sweet to know that God will hear
    The anxious soul's imploring prayer.

How sweet to lean upon that arm,
    And in its strength a refuge find;
Secure from every fear or harm,
    Which would disturb our peace of mind.

Jesus, thou Refuge ever sure,
    Where all is peace, and joy, and rest;
Safe as the rock that doth endure,
    Oh! let me lean upon Thy breast.

Then let the world its warfare wage,
    And Satan tempt my heart with pride;
Let friends disown, and scoffers rage,
    To turn my heart from Thee aside—

They all shall fail! but Thou alone
    Shalt be my portion evermore;
I'll cling to Thee—the world disown—
    Thy love confess—and Thee adore!

SACRED.

THE MISSIONARY'S PRAYER.

LORD, with thine arm support our cause,
While, in obedience to thy laws,
We raise Thy banner, plead Thy pow'r,
To save when in the trying hour.

Lord, send Thy soldiers to the field,
And make the pow'rs of Satan yield
To thy strong arm, that arm of might,
Which shieldeth those who do the right.

Lord, put Thy Word into our heart,
That we to others may impart
The knowledge of Thy saving grace,
To every tribe of every race!

Then shall we praise Thy mighty name,
And in all lands Thy right proclaim;
Where prayers of gratitude will rise,
Like grateful incense to the skies.

THE CHRISTIAN'S HOPE.

WE cannot meet with undimm'd eye
    The sun's effulgent, piercing rays;
No more can we, while 'neath the sky,
    Fathom our great Creator's ways.

Still let us search, with humble awe,
    And scan His wondrous works with care;
And round His glorious footstool draw
    In humble, pleading, fervent prayer:

That He who rules celestial spheres,
    And holds the oceans in His hand,
Would free our hearts from doubts and fears,
    And lead us to that glorious land,

Where doubts no more disturb the mind,
    And fears no more distress the heart;
Where we shall full fruition find,
    And kindred meet no more to part.

Oh! may we stand on heavenly ground,
    Where sweetest music charms the ear;
Where peace, and joy, and love abound—
    For God Himself is ever near.

Oh! glorious land of endless day,
    Oh! happy home so bright and fair;
Where saints unceasing homage pay
    To Him whose blood has brought them there.

THY CHOICE — WHICH?

OH! which shall I choose,
  Accept, or refuse,—
The pleasures of sin for a season?
  Or cling to the Cross,
  Through profit or loss,
Oh! tell me, and give me a reason?

  The reasons I give
  All others outlive,—
The pleasures of sin are deceiving;
  And soon pass away,
  Like winter's short day,
And leave the soul dark with its grieving:

  Then cling to the Cross,
  And count it not loss
To sacrifice earth's empty pleasure;
  Think nothing of pain,
  If Heaven thou gain,
And there have thy storehouse of treasure!

MY PORTION.

1. The Lord is my Portion, Then what need I fear? Though foes gather

round me, my Help - er is near; Let troubles as - sail me, or

dark storms a - rise, I'm safe on the "Strong Tower" that points to the skies.

THE Lord is my Portion, then what need I fear?
Though foes gather round me, my Helper is near;
Let troubles assail me or dark storms arise,
I'm safe on the " Strong Tower" that points to the skies.

The Lord is my Portion, the Lord is my Friend,
My hope from beginning, my joy to the end;
No other His place in my heart can supply,
Which wells with its fulness when Jesus is nigh.

The Lord is my Portion in life and in death,
In lisping His name I shall spend my last breath,
I'll praise Him for ever for thinking of me,
And dying to save me on Calvary's tree.

The Lord is my Portion,—earth's portion is vain,
'Tis burdened with sorrow, and sickness, and pain;
Oh! gladly I'll leave it on hearing His call,
Then prostrate before Him in gratitude fall!

THE TOUCH OF THE DIVINE.

EACH grain of sand by sounding sea,
   Each trembling leaf on quivering tree,
Each blade of grass on dewy lea,
     Speaks volumes of God's love to me!

The pearls that deep in ocean lie,
The twinkling stars that gem the sky,
The sunbeam, caught from noontide's eye,
     Direct my thoughts, oh God, to Thee!

The flowers that deck the fragrant dell,
And o'er me cast their beauty-spell,
I love them—for they seem to tell
     The story of God's love to me!

No matter where I wander free,
By river, lake, or boundless sea,
The touch of God's dear hand I see,
     And know by these He loveth me!

Oh, God! Thou doest all things well,
Earth, sea, and sky Thy wisdom tell,
In heaven what must it be to dwell
     For ever, O my God, with Thee!

CONSECRATION.

NOT my will, but Thine, O Lord!
Trusting to Thy promis'd Word;
Keep me ever near to Thee,
All through life my guardian be.
Teach me all I ought to know,
Guide me where I ought to go,
Be my Comforter and Friend,
Till I reach my journey's end!

Let my heart its fulness tell,
Gratitude my bosom swell;
Patient, humble, mild, and meek,
Let my lips Thy praises speak.
Darkness Thou hast turn'd to day,
Swept my guilty fears away;
Thou art all in all to me,—
I am naught compar'd to Thee!

When at last life's battle o'er,—
Landed safe on Canaan's shore,
I shall see Thy blessed face
Lighten up that glorious place;
Prostrate at Thy feet I'll fall,
There Thy wondrous love recall,—
Love so boundless, deep, and free,
That it compass'd—"EVEN ME!"

SACRED.

HYMN OF PRAISE.

THOU God that rulest earth and Heaven,
To Thee be praise and glory given;
Let all on earth behold Thy power
And goodness in each passing hour.

How shall we praise Thy matchless love
In Thy Son's mission from above?
Who came to raise a fallen race,
And fit them for a nobler place.

Oh, touch us all with holy fire,
Our breasts with gratitude inspire;
That we may teach all those who stray,
The narrow, sure, and only way.

Oh, keep us in the narrow road,
Until in Heaven we meet our God;
Then shall we endless praises sing,
And Heaven with "hallelujahs" ring!

THE HOUSE OF GOD.

HENCE! every thought of worldly care,
This is the House of God;
My soul, as for a feast prepare,
Thy burdens here unload.

The pealing organ sweetly rings
Its cadence everywhere;
From pew to pew bright angel-wings
Seem floating through the air!

Ah! God is here—how very near—
We speak to Him in prayer;
His voice so dear dispels our fear,
And soothes our every care.

From out His Holy Word we read
His promises secure;
"Yea and Amen" they are indeed,
And ever shall endure.

The man of God, with solemn voice,
Expounds "the message" given;
And as he speaks our hearts rejoice
As if approaching Heaven.

He dwells upon the love of God,
So boundless, pure, and free;
And of His Son, who bore the rod,
And died upon the tree.

SACRED.

The rich and poor, the young and old,
   Here like one family meet,—
One heavenly shepherd and one fold,
   And one communion sweet.

Dear day! the best of all the seven,
   My heart with rapture swells;
'Tis as the melody of Heaven,
   The sound of Sabbath bells!

Like doves unto their downy nest,
   Our souls fly out to thee:
Sweet foretaste of that heavenly rest
   For souls from sin set free.

THE CHRISTIAN'S ARMOUR.

Ephesians vi., 10—18.

OH! Christian brother! would'st thou know
From whence thy strength should be,
When wrestling with thy bitter foe,
Who seeks to conquer thee?

With might from God, the Lord, be strong,
And in His strength prevail;
With heavenly armour battle wrong,
And thou shalt never fail.

Thy loins be girt about with truth,
The truth of God is sure;
'Twill compass all the snares of youth,
And keep thee ever pure.

Let righteousness thy breastplate be,
To ward thee in the fight;
Love God and man—deep, strong, and free,
By morning, noon, and night.

Shod with the preparation
Of holy Gospel peace,
The footsteps of the godly man
From strength to strength increase.

The shield of faith, above all, see
That it be clear and bright;
From it the fiery darts shall flee,
And vanish from thy sight.

Salvation's helmet guards thy head,
  And shields from hurt thy face;
Inscribed upon it may be read:
  "A SINNER SAVED BY GRACE."

Thy right hand grasps the two-edged sword,
  With firmness and with might;
The true-dividing of God's Word
  Is justice, truth, and right.

Then polish up thy armour bright,
  With vigilance and care,
And thou shalt conquer in the fight,
  By patience, faith, and prayer.

Let prayer like incense ever rise
  To God from souls set free;
Until we gain the heavenly prize,
  And His own image see!

THE LORD'S PRAYER,
(PARAPHRASED).

1. " Our Father, which art in Heaven."
FATHER of Lights and God of Love,
 Thrice Holy is Thy name ;
Thou King of Kings, enthron'd above,
 Thou ever art the same.

2. " Hallowed be Thy name."
Forever hallowed be Thy name
 By hosts in earth and Heaven ;
In heathen lands make known Thy fame,
 And saving mercy given.

3. " Thy Kingdom come."
Thy kingdoms stretch from pole to pole,
 Throughout earth's utmost bound ;
Till gathered in each blood-bought soul,
 That on the earth is found.

4. " Thy will be done on earth as it is in Heaven."
Thy will be ours from morn till night,
 Obedient to Thy Word ;
Then shall our path be clear and bright,
 And sin shall be abhorr'd.

5. " Give us this day our daily bread."
That man shall nothing be denied,
 Who truly seeks Thy face ;
Our earthly wants are all supplied
 With bounty, love, and grace.

SACRED.

6. "*And forgive us our trespasses.*"
 Our sins and failures we confess,
  On bended knee entreat;
 Thus, trusting to Thy tenderness,
  We'll worship at Thy feet.

7. "*As we forgive them that trespass
  against us.*"
 And may Thy love our hearts incline,
  To mercy bend our ear;
 To pardon others who combine
  To cause us hurt or fear.

8. "*And lead us not into temptation,
  but deliver us from evil.*"
 From Satan's tempting snares of sin,
  Thy right hand shall deliver;
 Our God shall keep us pure within,
  Though Hell's foundations quiver.

9. '*For Thine is the Kingdom, the power,
  and the glory, for ever.*"
 Thine are the kingdoms of the earth,
  And thine the glory ever;
 This world did own Thee at her birth,
  Thou everlasting Giver.

10. "*Amen!*"
 Amen! Amen! so let it be,
  God's counsel faileth never;
 The Truth of God is pure and free,
  And shall prevail for ever!

THE LONGING SOUL.

OH! blessed Jesus, cast on me
   One look of pitying love;
That moment shall my soul be free,
   And sing with saints above.

Thy all-sufficient love is such
   That none need ever fear,
Or think that they can ask too much,
   Nor doubt Thy presence near.

In life or death, in weal or woe,
   In sunshine, shade, or shower,
To Thee in pray'r my thoughts shall go,
   And bless each passing hour.

Then, Saviour, teach me what Thou wilt,
   Oh, save me from my sin;
Cleanse Thou my soul from all its guilt,
   And make me pure within.

Then shall I walk with God on earth,
   And dwell with saints in Heaven;
Thus sanctify this second birth
   By saving mercy given.

OH! FAINTING HEART.

OH! fainting heart! why dost thou fear
　　The hour of dissolution?
'Tis then thy Saviour is most near,
　　To grant thee absolution.
The soul that rests on God shall live,
　　Through all earth's tribulation,
To His beloved He shall give
　　All needed consolation.

God hath sustained us all through life,
　　From infancy to manhood,
Then let us cease all needless strife,
　　His Word doth always stand good!
When passing through death's sullen stream,
　　His hand shall safely guide thee,
Behind the cloud there still doth gleam
　　The Light of Life beside thee.

Then look not back on things of earth,
　　Thy sins are all forgiven,
The fulness of thy second birth
　　Is registered in Heaven!
There, robes of spotless white are thine,
　　To cover doubts and fears;
God's everlasting arms entwine,
　　His hands shall wipe all tears.

STAND THOU THE TEST!

"I will refine them as silver is refined, and will try them as gold is tried, they shall call on My name, and I will hear them.—*Zech. xiii. 9.*

LET not your heart, my friend,
   Be troubled, nor afraid,
Thy God relief shall send,
   Trust, then, His promised aid;
     He doth not sleep,
     He will thee keep,
   If thou on Him doth stay
   He'll guide thee on thy way!

Trust not to self, my friend,
   But put thy trust in God;
Thy heart in meekness bend,
   Even 'neath His chastening rod:
     Stand thou the test,
     Tried gold is best,
   From dross and sin set free—
   The Master's image see!

SACRED.

Walk ever bravely on—
God is at thy right hand,
His strong arm lean upon—
Firm shalt thou ever stand;
By night or day
He knows the way,
He'll guide thee with His eye
Up to the realms on high!

Soon shall thy journey end
In perfect peace and love,
Where angels shall attend
And welcome thee above;
Life's race well run,
Well done! well done!
Thus enter into rest
Those that have stood the test!

"LORD, I BELIEVE!"

"LORD, I believe!" yet oft I fear,
    My faith is like the mustard seed;
'Tis then I pray that Thou be near—
    A present help in time of need!

"Lord, I believe" Thy promise true,
    That Thou art near to those who seek;
The fainting heart Thou wilt renew
    And words of heavenly comfort speak!

"Lord, I believe!" though vision fails
    To see the Hand that points the way;
That man who trusts in Thee prevails,
    Nor sin, nor death, o'er him holds sway!

"Lord, I believe" that Thou hast died
    To save me from the power of sin;
Then let me near to Thee abide
    Till Thou to glory draw me in!

BRING ANOTHER TO JESUS.

"And he brought him to Jesus."—*John i. 42.*

FIRST give thyself to Jesus,
    Then bring your nearest friend,
He beckons to receive us
    And loves us to the end;
Thus shall we haste the coming
    Of our dear absent Lord,
His love our souls consuming
    Shall magnify His Word.

Then still bring more to Jesus
    As jewels for His crown,
The world will soon believe us
    And lay its tribute down,
Exchanging doubt and sadness
    For Jesus' loving glance,
Our hearts shall sing with gladness
    To see His cause advance.

Then tell the love of Jesus
    O'er all the earth around,
No other hope could cheer us,
    No other help be found;
The One whom Satan feareth
    Shall come in power again,
When that glad day appeareth
    Our Lord and King shall reign!

THERE IS A GOD!

THERE is a God!—I know full well,
   Though I have never seen His face;
Earth, sea, and sky, His power tell,
   His handiwork in these I trace.

There is a God!—the heavens declare
   His gracious presence night and morn;
Sun, moon, and stars in God's pure air
   Laugh Infidelity to scorn.

There is a God!—each flower I see
   Seems but to live to speak His praise;
Each blade of grass, each leaf-crown'd tree,
   Their heads in grateful gladness raise!

There is a God!—thus saith the sea,
   Rock'd in the cradle of His hand;
Emblem of God's immensity,
   Mov'd by the winds at His command.

There is a God!—the mountains high
   Point to His heavenly throne above!
The stars that twinkle in the sky
   Proclaim a God—a God of love!

Thou art my God!—Thy word doth show
   The imprint of Thy hand divine;
'Tis from its pages that I know
   My soul is kindred soul to Thine!

SONNETS.

Sonnets.

THE LAST ENEMY — DEATH.

DEATH comes to all, no man can stay his hand;
If he but calls, the proudest in the land
His summons must obey, and then be led
By his cold, icy hand 'mong silent dead;
There to remain till Death himself shall die,
And He who conquered Death shall reign on high.
Oh, Death! where is thy sting if Jesus save?
Where, then, thy victory, O cruel grave?
Thou hast no power o'er him whom God defends,
For him all things subserve most glorious ends.
Death but relieves from earthly pain and woe,
A friend, though in the guise of mortal foe.
Oh, may the grave to me be but a door
To that bright land where Death shall reign no more!

THE MASTER'S CALL.

GO work to-day! the fields are white to view,
The harvest truly great, the labour'rs few;
To you the call is giv'n, reapers, obey!
Work mightily, while yet 'tis called to-day!
The night approacheth when no man can work,
And sin and vice do in the darkness lurk.
The fields are many and the world is wide,
O'er trackless forests, deserts, stormy tide
Proclaim that love which makes all mankind kin,
And saves the soul though steep'd in direst sin;
Which frees the captive, gladdens the oppress'd,
And leads the erring to the Saviour's breast;
Where pard'ning mercy, love, and joy are giv'n
To make this earth a sweet foretaste of Heaven.

SONNETS.

THE SABBATH SCHOOL TEACHER'S REWARD.

OH, teacher, faint not! thou art not alone,
He who hath called thee will thy labour own;
And though, at first, no grateful fruit appear,
Think not 'tis labour lost, but persevere;
Yield not the conflict to the Master's foe,
But still "from strength to strength" unwearied go.
Plant thou the seeds of heav'nly truth with care,
And water oft with fervent, pleading prayer,
Then leave the rest to God, whose Spirit's power
Shall cause the seed to grow, the plant to flower,
Till in due course the ripen'd fruit appears
To cheer thy heart, reward thy prayers and tears,
And make thee sing for joy,—that peace bestow
Which they who serve the Lord alone doth know.

A PRAYER FOR WISDOM.

1 Kings iii., 11, 12; Prov. iii., 13—18.

OH! let me ever walk in Wisdom's way,
That I may wiser grow, and day by day
Prove that her paths are pleasantness and peace;
And, therein walking, may my years increase
In fruitful days of labour and reward,
Of love, and joy, and peace, and sweet concord.
Grant me the work which angels most enjoy,—
A life well spent in Heaven's blest employ,
In deeds of love, and works of holy zeal,
And in that occupation may I feel
The kind approval of a God of grace,
Who owns his servants with a smiling face;
My work accepted, and my sins forgiv'n,
Bless'd while on earth, and doubly bless'd in Heaven.

JESUS, MY REFUGE.

"A hiding place from the wind and a covert from the tempest; as the shadow of a great rock in a weary land."
—Isa. xxxii. 2.

OH, grateful shelter from the storms of life,
From cares corroding or from worldly strife;
Fain would my panting soul Thy shadow seek,
And, shielded safe, in grateful accents speak
Of all Thy love to man, whose strength Thou art,
Whose refuge sure, the uplifter of the heart
Of him who strives to seek Thy safe retreat,
And loves with Thee to dwell—there at Thy feet
Lay sorrow's burden down; Thy gracious gift
Accepts with thankful heart, nor seeks to lift
With sinful hands once more the heavy load
That bars the soul's communion with his God;
Ah! there would I in calm repose abide,
Safe as The Rock near which I seek to hide.

CHRISTIAN, AWAKE!

CHRISTIAN, awake! thy life is not a dream,
You cannot glide for ever with the stream :
'Tis like the ocean in her changing moods
Of great uproar, or calm, deep solitudes;
Her varying tides a ceaseless motion keep,
And danger ever haunts the mighty deep;
Yet o'er her bosom in majestic pride
The noble vessel doth in safety ride,
Defying all the stormy winds that blow,—
Making a highway of a raging foe,
Till the bright haven doth appear in view,
Which speaks of rest to all the weary crew ;
Where, sails all furl'd, anchor firm and fast,
They rest the sweeter for the dangers past!

THE NAME OF JESUS.

SWEET name! what cadence in the very sound!
What heav'nly music in the utt'rance found,
When whisper'd in the ear of dying saint,
Tho' spent with pain, and pulse and heart beat faint;
Yet, at the name of "JESUS" doth his eyes
Seek ours in love, and peace, and glad surprise,
And then forever close in sweet content
To open them in Heav'n—a life well spent!
Oh, Jesus! Thine the ever-potent power
To charm, to heal, to bless, in trial's hour;
Let all the world Thy name with rev'rence hear,
And trust Thy pow'r to save; with holy fear
Approach the footstool of Thy matchless grace,
And find in Thee their soul's dear resting-place!

THE SABBATH-DAY.

SWEET day of rest! most precious of the seven,
God's gracious gift to man, in mercy giv'n
That he may cease from toil and worldly care,
And for that brighter rest his soul prepare.
Blest harbinger of that eternal day,
Whose beams shall never fade or pass away.
Oh, may we ever watch with jealous eye,
And careful guard the hours that swiftly fly,
That nought but heav'nly themes our thoughts engage,
And with temptation hourly warfare wage;
Oft by " the footsteps of the flock " be found,
Within the house of God, on praying ground,
And there our grateful hearts shall homage pay,
To Him who rose triumphant on that day.

THE IMAGE OF THE HEAVENLY.

ALMIGHTY God! in all Thy works display'd,
For man in Thine own image Thou hast made;
How should we, then, Thine every law respect,
And mourn in dust and ashes if neglect
Of ours should once but mar that Image bright,
And, grieving Thee, turn sunshine into night.
Let not our hearts from Thee be turn'd aside,
But let Thy Holy Spirit with us 'bide;
Then shall our life be like the flowers in June,
Displaying sweetness, and our hearts in tune
To the pure melodies of heav'nly song,
Which to the ransom'd hosts of Heav'n belong;
Thus here below let glorious anthems rise
To mingle with the songs of Paradise.

THE PEACE OF GOD.

THERE is a peace the world can not bestow
Nor take away; and they in joy do go
Who but possess it, for its charm is sure,
And doth through all the ills of life endure;
It makes the soul rejoice, the weak feel strong,
The troubled soul burst forth in joyous song,
Which may be heard above the din of strife,—
An antidote for all the cares of life!
Oh! peace of God! may I thy pow'r enjoy,
Then in thy praise my life shall find employ;
Thou shalt me 'fend from every evil way,
Make all my darkness turn to brightest day,
Till, safe within the everlasting arms,
My soul shall rest secure from all alarms!

CONSCIENCE.

CONSCIENCE is the true monitor of God
For our approval, or a very rod
Of direst chastisement for evil deeds,
Or wicked thoughts that grow like noxious weeds
Within the garden of the human heart,
To mar the buds and flowers which would impart
A fragrant solace to the weary soul
Of God-made man, thus strengthen and control
His better nature in Temptation's day,
And drive the hateful thoughts of sin away,
To hide themselves for very shame of sin,
And, hence renewed, the better life begin:
Thus, Conscience, listened to, will safely guide
Where perfect peace and happiness abide!

SEEKING AFTER KNOWLEDGE.

WISDOM is the true currency of Heaven,
From fools withheld, but to the prudent given;
In her pursuit let us in earnest be.
If we would prosper, therefore, let us see
That all our energies be so combin'd
As best to cultivate the heart and mind.
This occupation is the best that can
Engage the youth, or occupy the man
In leisure hours, which, be they rightly spent,
Are of great moment, and by Heaven lent
To sweeten toil, and relaxation give
To dull and cank'ring cares, which, while we live,
Must be our lot; our time, then, let us spend
As best becomes us, knowing not our end!

"FAITH, HOPE AND CHARITY."

"THESE THREE."

FAITH is the starting-point to higher ground,
   Each step—sure-footed—on THE ROCK is found;
No backward gazing at our former fears,
But stronger growing as recede the years!
HOPE is the telescope that scans afar,—
Each heavenly thought seems like a new-found star!
Though for a season bound by earth's employ,
Hope sings on earth sweet heavenly songs of joy!
SWEET CHARITY! true bond of love and peace,
Thy kindly counsel maketh strife to cease;
Thou rulest with a loving, gentle hand,
And, smiling, points us to the better land!
FAITH, HOPE and CHARITY! oh, truth sublime,
These three shall bridge us o'er the sea of Time.

PLEADING.

OH! theme of wondrous power!—with God to
    plead—
And speak to Him in our great times of need!
With faith's bright eye peer through earth's darkest
    night
And read the meaning of the Infinite!
Oh! gift of gifts! to erring mortals given—
Kneeling on earth, yet, kneeling, soar to heaven!
To lisp and stammer, yet prevail with God
To turn aside from us His chastening rod!
More liberty with God than angels know
Have they who seek His ear in time of woe!
Claiming the merits of a Saviour's love
To gain a hearing in the courts above!
He who doth mark each sparrow's fall with care
Counts all tears and answers fervent prayer!

INFIDELITY.

'TIS foolish to affirm "there is no God,"
   When all around us lie the evidence :
The smallest flower that gems the verdant sod
   Speaks to us mutely of His Providence;
The starry firmament proclaims His might
   While it defies our finite minds to know
The why and wherefore of the Infinite,
   And all our calculations overthrow!
Oh! puny man! why dost thou upright walk
   While other creatures crawl, or lowly bend,
As if in awe of God?—yet dost thou talk
   Of wisdom, power, and knowledge without end!
Infidelity is spiritual blindness,—
   God all around—yet will not Him confess!

RESIGNATION.

"THY will be done!"—though mine be all
    undone;
Thou art the Fashioner—I but the clay:
Then mould me as Thou wilt from day to day
Until my course on earth be fully run.
'Tis not for me to say—"What doest Thou?"
    Thou doest all things well: Thy name is Love!
    Thine aim to fit me for Thy courts above:
Then stamp Thine image fair upon my brow!
'Tis mine to only wait, and watch, and pray
    To be preserved from evil and from sin,
    And let Thy Spirit rule my heart within,
Trusting Thee fully even though Thou slay!
    Come life or death—come happiness or woe—
    Mine but to follow where Thou'dst have me go!

THY LAST HOUR.

OH, think of it! for it shall surely come,—
  Thy last lone hour on earth, when thou must part
With all thou holdest dear within thy heart,
And death's great loneliness shall strike thee dumb
Yet, let not dark despair thy heart enshroud,—
A ray of light rims even this dismal cloud;
If thou dost look for it, thy soul shall see
Beyond the tomb a haven of repose
Prepared, in love, by God for such as thee;
For those who trust in Jesus mercy flows!
Thus may thy setting sun on earth but be
A harbinger of better things for thee;
For, ere to-morrow's earthly sun doth rise
Thy ransom'd soul may mount to Paradise.

LIGHT.

GOD said: "Let there be light," and from the sky
Shone forth the "ruler of the day" on high.
To rule the darkness of chaotic night
He sent the moon forth with her silvery light.
Soon countless stars peep'd out as if to see
The new creation in its infancy!
Then God made man in His own image fair,
And gave him Eve his earthly joys to share;
But man's sad fall from purity and grace
Brought spiritual darkness o'er the human race.
"I AM THE LIGHT," our blessed Saviour said,
And meekly bow'd for us His holy head;
A heavenly light He shed o'er life's dark way,
Shining more bright as nears the perfect day!

SONNETS.

TRUTH.

TRUTH is that spotless purity of soul
　　Which seeks the light, and loves to bask
　therein!
Not truth in part—then silence, but the whole
　　Unvarnished facts, without one taint of sin!
Such is the standard of the living God,
　　Before whom all that dares to lie must fall,
Feeling their conscience, like a heated rod,
　　Forever searing and consuming all!
Truth stands the test of torture, fire or sword,
　　And from them all comes forth the more refined.
When fixed upon God's everlasting Word,—
　　Truth to all subtlety and art is blind;
Though tempted sore, yet utter not a lie,
For God and Truth brave men have dar'd to die!

HOPE DEFERRED!

'TIS hope deferred—life's lamp goes out at
   night—
One flicker more and all is darkness deep,
Made all the darker as the hopes were bright;
   The more of joy we miss the more we weep,
As hope departs and leaves but blank despair,
   Then weeping ceases for the lack of power!
The Winter of the soul has come!—and bare
   Are all the branches of the tree, whose flower
Gave promise of such benisons of bliss,
   That each glad leaf was hailed with new delight
By sun and shower, and dew-drop's hopeful kiss,
   And all seemed fair each morning, noon, and
   night!
But fruit came not; and leaf by leaf decayed;
Then sank my heart and sought Death's grateful
   shade!

CHRISTMAS GIFTS.

OH! happy eve! that ushers in the day
   Of all the year the best to young and old!
This night our thoughts take wings and soar away
  To Bethlehem's plains, where shepherds tend their fold.
Angelic strains are borne upon the wind
  Of "peace on earth, good-will to all mankind;"
See! yonder star of promise that doth bring
Our eager footsteps to earth's new-born king,
There pay we homage to the Holy Child
Born in a manger—'mid surroundings wild—
Where "wise men from the East" pour at His feet
Earth's finest gold—all spices rare and sweet!
OH! LET OUR CHRISTMAS OFFERINGS EVER BE
A PORTION OF OUR BEST, O LORD, TO THEE!

SUNRISE!

NATURE rejoices in a thousand ways
    When first the morning sunlight westward
  streams;
Sunward the birds pour forth their joyous lays
    And, singing, wake us from morn's fitful dreams;
Under thy warmth the flowers expand and look
    With smiling eyes toward thy welcome rays;
While river, mountain, plain, and purling brook
    Sing tunefully in chorus to thy praise!
Oh, blessed sunlight!—emblem of that Light
    Which lighteth our dark souls with heavenly
  love;
May we expand and grow with glad delight
    As doth the flowers that smile and look above!
Oh, Father! let the light from Jesus' face
Illume our hearts and there His image trace!

WHAT IS REGRET?

A sombre shadow o'er life's pleasant way—
  A pain one feels yet cannot well express;
A mis-spent moment of a well-spent day—
  A thoughtless act too late to make redress;
A hasty word we fain had never said,
  A dark'ning cloud where sunshine might have been;
A drooping eye, a lowly bowed head,—
  These are the symptoms of Regret, I ween.
Let us be watchful over every act,
  And ponder well the path we seek to tread;
One thoughtless action may life's good detract,
  Our influence mar long after we are dead!
Hedge well thy ways with watchfulness and pray'r,
Thus 'void Regret—twin-sister to Despair!

MOTHER-LOVE.

SEE yonder mother with her sickly child
   Pressed closely to her heaving, anxious breast,
For many days and nights forebodings wild
   Have fill'd her heart and banished needful rest;
Yet, at the faintest cry or wish exprest,
   She gladly seeks to soothe its every pain,
   And, if succesful, thinks it purest gain
Ere to her own great need comes fitful rest!
Oh! mother-love! great waters cannot quench
   Nor flames deter thee from thy patient zeal;
Thy love-strong hands grim prison-bars would wrench,
   There with thy suffering child at home to feel;
   The purest love on earth is mother-love,
   Full kin to that made manifest above!

SLEEP.

SLEEP, blessed Sleep! of comforters the best,
　　Thou " sweet restorer " of a wearied frame;
In thy embrace we gladly sink to rest,
　　And thus forget earth's fickle praise or blame!
Or, in our dreams, revisit other lands
　　Where first our happy childhood's years were spent,
And join in playful glee our toil-worn hands
　　In youthful happiness and sweet content;
Or kneel beside a godly mother's knee
　　And lisp again our evening prayer sublime,
And feel, from all earth's care and trouble free,
　　The flowery freshness of life's glad spring-time!
Sleep's but the emblem of our long last rest,
If pillow'd safely on our Saviour's breast!

PATIENCE.

PATIENCE! thou art a giant in thy strength,
    A miracle of wonder-working power;
By calm endurance success crowns at length
    As certain as the fruit succeeds the flower!
Patience—brave heart! 'tis step by step we go
    And reach at last the haven of our hopes!
'Tis drop by drop—then hidden springs o'erflow
    And rush in torrents down the mountain slopes!
'Tis one by one our moments swiftly fly
    To form the deathless history of the past!
Then patiently pursue thy purpose high
    While genius, hope, and emulation last.
Patience is true greatness?—e'en though defeat
Seem imminent, yet patience still is sweet!

PERSEVERANCE.

DISAPPOINTMENT is not utter failure,
    The striving is a measure of success;
Each wise attempt but makes us stronger grow,
    Till, oft-repeated, stumbling-blocks seem less,
And finally prove stepping-stones to gain
The end in view, and our fond hopes attain!
As drops of water wear the solid rock,
    Or sun's bright ray, in focus, kindle flame,
So concentrated effort, wisely spent,
    Will yet be crowned with success and with fame!
If that thy aim be good, then persevere,
Though success fail thee, this thy heart may cheer:
No man e'er strove with noble end in view,
But from the strife came forth more brave and true!

FREEDOM.

FREEDOM is obedience to righteous law
   Framed for the guidance of a nation great;
Made to be kept—not broken by a flaw
   Known only to the rulers of the State!
Justice that treats the rich and poor alike,
   Defending each from favor or attack;
Slow to convict—yet ready aye to strike
   The fatal blow on all that honor lack!
A nation's strength is measured by her laws;
   Her safety is the welfare of her sons;
Industry and loyalty the power that draws
   In peace her commerce, and in war her guns!
Freedom—our birthright, sell it not for gold,
Our fathers bought it with their blood of old!

LIBERTY.

SWEET LIBERTY!—thou birthright of mankind,
Yet which some autocrats would fain destroy!
How like our God to give!—like man to take
What God hath given so freely in his love
To make our life on earth more bearable!
Though man loves liberty, yet—miser-like—
Seeks to withhold it from his fellow-man,
And, boasting, pride himself in larceny!
Go to! thou false vile traitor to thy race,
Thy stony heart is index'd on thy face!
While loving Liberty thyself—deny
To those within thy power their liberty!
The soul that seeks to bind his fellow man
May soon be measured by an infant's span!

FRIENDSHIP.

FRIENDSHIP! thou holy bond that binds my
    heart
To others that to mine seem counterpart,—
Love-giving, yet love-getting all the more,
Thus daily adding to our mutual store
Of kindly deeds and words, each thought and look
As readable and clear as printed book;
Enjoyable in life's gay, golden hour,
Yet doubly so when clouds of trial lower;
Then closer draw, as lambs do in the fold,
To gather heat, and 'scape the rain and cold,
Till warmth and sunshine take the place of rain,
Then off they gambol on the hills again!
Oh! Friendship! thou art like a golden chain,
Each link a friend—each friend a golden gain!

WHAT IS JOY?

JOY is the constant outflow of a heart
    Full of its happiness and ecstasy!
Pure as a mountain spring; born to impart
    Its healthy sweetness o'er life's dusty way!
Refreshing hearts o'erfraught with worldly care—
    Laughing and skipping like a child at play,
Wooing the flowers that seem to it most fair—
    No morrow clouds the brightness of to-day!
Joy is the language that the angel's know,
    And teach the infant at its mother's breast,
Whose dimpled cheeks with sun-lit smiles overflow,
    While fondled safely in the parent nest!
Joy! like the music of the birds in spring,
Make other hearts with joyous rapture sing!

VICTORIA'S JUBILEE.—1887.

WHAT means this shout of joy o'er all the
    earth?—
A nation's thankfulness ! a nation's praise !
From whence the cause that gives such joy its birth,
    And o'er the world such great commotion raise ?
For fifty years our noble Queen hath stood
    The trying ordeal of a nation's crown !
Beloved by all—" Victoria, the good,"
    On freedom smiled—gave slavery her frown !
All through her lonely years of widowhood
    She held with dignity a nation's rein :
Was ever Queen so well-belov'd and good ?
    Did ever king such lasting homage gain ?
Victoria !—as Mother, Queen or Wife,
Thou has adorn'd thy pathway all through life !

MUSIC.

WHEN music takes possession of the heart,
    A coward well may act a hero's part,
And dare the deadly trenches of the foe—
With valiant comrades strike the victor's blow!
And when in happy "piping times of peace"
    Glad lovers meet to join the merry dance,
    At sound of music each bright eye doth glance
With love and joy, nor tire till music cease!
Sweet music is the language of the soul,
    It calms the weeping infant of a day,
    And soothes the aged saint at life's decay,
Like healing balm, makes wounded spirits whole!
Celestial music!—boon to man on earth!
Thy angel-tones hath surely heavenly birth!

TEARS.

TEARS are the outflow of great joy or grief,
　　The speechless language of a swelling heart,
Whose fitful solace is a sure relief
　　For joys excessive, or affliction's smart;
The valve-escapement of a pent-up soul,
　　Whose fulness finds expression in a tear;
Which, like healing balm, makes the wounded whole;
　　Or dearest friend—when darkest hour is near—
Whose hands we clasp in friendship's sacred hold,
　　And cling to them like ivy round the tree,—
Weakness and strength combined in love's enfold,—
　　Then let the flood-gates open full and free!
Our bitter tears but give us strength to bear
Affliction sore, or joy's too sudden glare!

THE DRUNKARD'S FATE.

FOR the drunkard there's no such place as "home,"
Though over the face of the earth he roam,
Till Death shall unfetter the drink-bound slave,
And he findeth " rest " in the silent grave;
His untimely death—" the wages of sin,"—
Satan's reward for the worship of Gin!
He gave up his wife and his children dear
For the drink which he thought his heart could cheer;
But the more he drank the lower he sank,
From the highest grade to the lowest rank,
Till for shame, his name a bye-word became,
And he lost for ever his once fair name :—
For the pleasure of drink, which he loved so well,
He barter'd his soul to the lowest hell!

PAIN!

WE shrink and recoil at the touch of Pain,
Yet know that escape from his grasp is vain;
And our trembling hearts with emotion swell
As we sigh and groan at each painful spell;
But the dreadful hour of suffering past,
And our courage and health restored at last,
How soon we forget our terror and pain,
And mingle once more with the world again;
But not as before, for a tender string
Hath been set to music, and thus doth sing:
I have suffered, and feel for others' pain
A twinge of my own past sorrow again!
Ah! Pain, what a useful teacher thou art,
Lessons of sympathy thus to impart!

WHAT IS LOVE?

LOVE is the grateful off'ring of a heart
In all its fulness to some counterpart,—
Zeal answering zeal, each striving to excel,
Zealous to share the glowing thoughts that dwell
In hearts united by Love's silken bands,
Each thread some joy Love only understands.
'Mid stirring echoes of a fond desire
Claim kindred feelings and a sister-fire,
Joining life's hopes in one ecstatic song,
As sweetest music from an angel-throng;
No doubt or fear disturbs Love's peaceful rest,
Nor cares corroding rankle in her breast;
Each thought bears fruit in others sweeter still,
Till earth seems heav'n, and heav'n seems own'd at will.

"IN A MOMENT."

A STREET SCENE.

"IN A MOMENT"—full prone upon the ground
The lifeless body of a man was found;
Without one word of parting or regret
His sudden and untimely death he met;
Yet died as he had lived—trustful in God
And ready even to kiss the chastening rod
That called him "in a moment" to depart
And be with Him who binds the troubled heart,
O'er-wrought with labor and surcharged with care,
Sustained thus far through faith and secret prayer,
To Him who knows the frailties of our frame,
Yet pardons all who trust in His sweet name!
In a moment translated in His love,
By one sharp pain, to endless bliss above!

RETALIATION.

OH, Canada! arise in thy young strength,
  And prove thyself a nation of the earth,
Whose veins are filled with blood of noble birth
That shall be honored, known and felt at length!
Think not of war!—but all that makes for peace
Be thine; thy aim—advancement and increase
In all that tends to make a nation great,
And thus be trained to cope with any fate!
Oh, may thy brother " 'cross the lines " be such
As brother ought to be to sister fair—
Two of one family—ask we thus too much
That God's free gifts they each alike may share?
Then should a foe our continent invade,
Brother and sister join in mutual aid!

SONNETS.

REST!

REST is the peaceful calm which follows toil:
Sweet to the labouring man who tills the soil;
Likewise most precious to the weary brain,
Tired with the dull routine of loss or gain;
Or to the authors of our learned books,
Who show the trace of study in their looks—
All value rest—all need those quiet hours
As much as doth the plant those welcome show'rs
Which Heaven sends to cool the fevered earth,
And cause sweet Nature sing aloud with mirth.
When God at first created earth and skies,
He "rested" in the shades of Paradise!
Likewise shall we, earth's care and labour o'er,
Find rest the sweeter for the toils we bore!

SONNETS.

THE SCENES OF EARLY YEARS!

'TIS sweet to visit scenes of early years,
　　After long absence on a foreign soil,
Where fortune hath rewarded patient toil
And lent glad wings to travel well-known ways,
Rich with the memory of bye-gone days
　　When budding life was like an opening flower,
　　Full of fair promise for each future hour,
And hope sang songs of ecstasy and praise,
　　Whose echoes still are ringing through the years
That bridge the early with the later days.
　　And I am young again with all that cheers
　　The exile's heart and eyes 'mid scenes of home!
Oh! scenes of early years that doth entwine
A potent spell round this fond heart of mine.

TORONTO.

FAIR Toronto! Queen City of the West !
Of other cities thou to me art best :
As far as eye can reach, from Don to Humber,
Are chimneys, tow'rs, and spires in goodly number,—
Cathedrals, churches, schools, and mansions rise,
In stately grandeur, tow'ring to the skies,
A noble harbour fronts thy southern bound,
And gentle hills encircle thee around;
From North to South, and East to West expand
Streets, Avenues, and Roads, so wisely plann'd
That strangers visit thee with ease, and find
In thee a home at once just to their mind ;
Long live Toronto ! loud her praises swell,
Here Commerce, Art, and Nature love to dwell !

SONNETS.

TORONTO BAY.

OH, lovely scene of ever-changing hue!
Dark ocean-green, or sky-bright azure-blue;
Swift o'er thy heaving bosom gaily float,
The trim-built yacht, gay skiff, or pleasure-boat;
Or, here and there, a light birch-bark canoe
Lends a romance to the enchanting view.
Toronto Island, in the distance, seems
The happy fairy-land of boyhood's dreams,
Where naught but Pleasure dwells, and music fills
The balmy air with melody that thrills
Each bounding heart with ecstasy and joy,
And happiness the fleeting hours employ!
Toronto Bay, by morning, noon, or night,
Thy waters charm me with some new delight!

ADIEU!

READER, "Adieu!"—I will not say "farewell!"
That word, full-fraught with sorrow as a knell,
Breathes forth a strain of sadness to mine ear,
And is too often mother to a tear!
"Adieu!" speaks hopeful that we yet may meet
And with each other hold communion sweet.
If aught that I have said doth give thee cheer
I've made a friend of thee—and friends are dear!
In this stern world of ours each friend we gain
Makes life more sweet, and helps to soothe life's pain!
Remember, then, dear friend, before we part,
These simple strains are from a glowing heart
That seeks to find an echo to its voice
In heart of thine—and, finding that, rejoice!

ALPHABETICAL INDEX.

ALPHABETICAL INDEX.

	PAGE.
A Birthday Greeting..	167
A Birthday Wish	266
A Bouquet of Flowers	90
Absent Sunday-School Teacher, (The)	242
A Bunch o' Heather..	70
Adieu	340
A Christmas Carol	163
African Slave Trade, (The)	244
A Golden Wedding ..	130
A Husband's Birthday Greeting	136
A Kiss through the Telephone	117
A Lesson from the Clock	175
An Anxious Soul Comforted	270
An Honest Man	181
A Prayer	269
A Prayer for Wisdom	300
A Scotch Suprise Party	254
A Souvenir of Love	97
A Summer's Day—	
Morning ..	151
Noon	153
Night	154
A Tribute to Mother	133
A Wife's Last Good-Bye	138
Baby's Portrait, (The) ..	121
Battle of Life, (The)	220
Believer's Refuge, (The)	274
Betrothed	146

INDEX.

	PAGE.
Bitter or the Sweet, (The)	213
Bonnets o' Glengarry, (The)	56
Bonnie Arran Hills, (The)	238
Bring Another to Jesus	293
British Arms, (The)	67
Brose, Parritch, Kail, Haggis, an' Bannocks	81
Brotherhood of Man, (The)	217
Bruce and Bannockburn	78
Buried in Her Cradle	256
Canada	73
Canada's Defenders	32
Canadian Nation, (The)	65
Christian's Armour, (The)	284
Christian, Awake	302
Christian's Hope, (The)	276
Christmas Gifts	317
Come Unto Me	271
Conscience	307
Consecration	280
Cross'd Love	143
Dead-Beat, (The)	214
Dinna Hide the Heart-love	148
Drunkard's Fate, (The)	331
Drunkard, (The)	252
Dying Child, (The)	204
Dying Scot Abroad, (The)	49
Eight-Hour Movement, (The)	216
Emblems of Friendship	99
Eyes that Speak	101
Faith, Hope and Charity	309
Faith Illustrated	165
Farewell	264
Flower of the Family, (The)	108
Flowers	168

INDEX.

	PAGE.
Fragments for Autograph Albums	266
Freedom	324
Friendship *(Sonnet)*	326
Friendship	266
Golden Rule, (The)	234
Good-Bye	262
Hame—Yet No at Hame	76
Happy Childhood	193
Happy Heart, (The)	209
Heart Questionings	86
Hielan' Fling (The)	68
His Only Pair of Pants	223
Hope Deferred	316
House of God, (The)	282
Humber " Fairy," (The)	95
Hymn of Praise	281
Image of the Heavenly, (The)	305
I Miss a Dear Face	135
In a Moment	334
Infidelity	311
Is This Life Worth Living?	231
Jesus' Love	273
Jesus, My Refuge	301
John Three-Sixteen	248
Jubilee Song	58
Knights of Labor, (The)	189
Knights of Pythias	194
Last Enemy—Death, (The)	297
Laughing	180
Learning the Twins to Walk	123
Liberty	325
Life's Brighter Side	190

INDEX.

	PAGE.
Life's Progress	173
Life's Supreme Moments	156
Light	314
Little Newspaper Boys, (The)	184
Longing Soul, (The)	288
Lord, I believe	292
Lord's Prayer, (The)	286
Love and Charity	93
Love and Sympathy	208
Love-Links	107
Lover's Ideal, (The)	120
Loves of an Infant-Class Scholar, (The)	243
Love's Progress	105
Master's Call, (The)	298
Missionary's Prayer, (The)	275
Misunderstood	124
Mortgaging the Homestead	258
Motherless Child, (The)	128
Mother-Love	320
Mother's Voice	141
Music	329
My Heart is Scotland's Yet..	53
My Mither's Grave	228
My Portion	278
Mystery	176
Name of Jesus, (The)	303
Nature's Temple..	160
Niagara Falls..	26
Nursery Clock, (The)	246
Ode to Lake Ontario	43
Oh! Fainting Heart	289
Old Year and the New, (The)	210
On a Visit to the Old Country	74
On My Fortieth Birthday	206
Our Baby	126

INDEX.

	PAGE.
Our Faither Abune	230
Our Johnnie	111
Our Native Land—Fair Canada	19
Pain	332
"Papa's Pet"	113
Patience	322
Peace of God, (The)	306
Pereseverance	323
Pleading	310
Power of Song, (The)	182
Preacher's Warning, (The)	272
Pride	207
Queenston Heights	38
Queen Victoria's Jubilee	37
Resignation	312
Rest	336
Retaliation	335
Romping with the Children	109
Rosedale	186
Sabbath Chimes	237
Sabbath-day, (The)	304
Sabbath School Teacher's Reward, (The)	299
Scarboro' Heights	253
Scenes of Early Years	337
Scotch Dainties	81
"Scotty."	34
Seeking after Knowledge	308
She Pays Her Debts with Kisses	200
Skating	247
Sleep	321
Soap-Bubbles	191
Song of Freedom	23
Song of the Drummer	170

INDEX.

	PAGE.
Sons of England..	63
Sons of Scotland	40
Stand Thou the Test	290
Star of Love, (The) ..	88
Sunday-School Infant Class, (The)	240
Sunrise	318
Sweetest Word on Earth is Home, (The)	51
Tears ..	330
Tender Passion, (The) ..	144
The Dominion of Canada ..	30
The Links that Bind Us	29
There is a God	294
The Thistle	44
Thy Choice—Which?	277
Thy Last Hour ..	313
To a Brother Bard ..	260
Tobogganing Song	233
Toddlin' Hame	226
To Glasgow, Scotland ..	46
To-Morrow ..	235
To My Friends ..	131
Toronto	338
Toronto Bay	339
To the Four Winds of Heaven	188
To the Pansy	174
Touch of the Divine, (The)	279
True Love	91
Truth ..	315
Two Poor Orphan Boys..	178
Victoria's Jubilee—1887	328
Voyage of Life, (The) ..	212
Welcome Home, Brave Volunteers!	24
What can Love Do?	103
What is Joy? ..	327

INDEX.

	PAGE.
What is Love?	333
What is Regret?	319
What Shall I Sing?	225
When Jesus was Away	250
When Love is King	232
Where Doth Beauty Dwell?	85
Workingman's Half-Holiday, (The)	202
Workingman's Wife, (The)	147
Yachting Song	219
Young Canada!	60
Young Musician, (The)	197

www.ingramcontent.com/pod-product-compliance
Lightning Source LLC
Chambersburg PA
CBHW030324240426
43673CB00040B/1264